The Preacher's Edge

JERRY L. SCHMALENBERGER

CSS Publishing Company, Inc.
Lima, Ohio

Library of Congress Cataloging-in-Publication Data

Schmalenberger, Jerry L.
    The preacher's edge / Jerry L. Schmalenberger.
        p.   cm.
    Includes bibliographical references.
    ISBN 0-7880-0767-X
    1. Preaching. I. Title.
BV4211.2.S367   1996
251—dc20   96-7934
                                                                                    CIP

0-7880-0767-X

This book is dedicated to the memory of Paul R. Brees and G. Vernon Kelley, professors of speech at Wittenberg University, Springfield, Ohio, who shaped my communication skills.

Acknowledgement

I would like to thank Lisa Dahlen for the many hours she spent assisting in the typing and editing of this book, and Carol Schmalenberger for the final editing and proofreading of the galley sheets.

Thanks also to Professor George Ramsay of Wittenberg University for drawing the three illustrations.

Table of Contents

The Delivery

Sample Sermons

Self-Help For The Preacher

Foreword

The famous sixteenth century reformer Martin Luther advised: "He who teaches most simply, childishly, popularly . . . that's the best preacher. I like it to be easy and earthy. But now if it is debate you're looking for, come into my classroom!"[1]

So this book is a plea for a preaching "close to the ground," using the very best speech techniques that have been discovered over the years. It is my best effort to move beyond correct sermons to vitally interesting ones.

Many Christians speak of the real presence of Christ in the sacraments of holy communion. Can we not rediscover Christ's real presence in the preaching event as well? And in a day when preaching, as well as preacher, may be taking its share of public ridicule, I want to reaffirm that it's an honorable thing to do and be — a preacher.

Some ideas I try to support in this book for preachers:

•The Bible gives strong affirmation to preaching.

•We can build effective preaching by paying attention to our listeners' reaction.

•The extended metaphor is one of the best ways of organizing and delivering our sermons.

•Public speaking technique has much to teach us about the delivery of our message.

•There are some ways we may be working against ourselves.

•We can preach on controversial subjects and financial stewardship and not drive our people away.

•Local history is a rich source of Gospel parable available to us.

•Baby boomers and busters demand new ways of preaching.

•We have an edge on any other speaker because of God's help with the sermon and with those who listen to our sermons.

•Intentional work on your preaching over a period of time can make a big difference in the effectiveness of the preaching event.

•The preacher's physical and spiritual health is crucial to dynamic preaching.

I have been brave enough to include three sample sermons where I have tried to "practice what I preach."

I have also included a ten week prescription for preaching improvement which a small group of lay people and the preacher can do together. I promise you and your congregation a wonderful experience if you will try it. Perhaps it can then be said of you, "To preach is to tread again with the congregation the way of the witness taken by the text."[2]

Again, from the famous reformer, the great preacher of his day, Martin Luther:

> *Pray that God will give you a mouth and to your audience ears . . . you will most certainly find out three things: First you will have prepared your sermon as diligently as you know how, and it will slip through your fingers like water; secondly, you may abandon your outline and God will give you grace. You will preach your very best. The audience will be pleased but you won't. And thirdly, when you have been unable in advance to pull anything together you will preach acceptably both to your hearers and to yourself. So pray to God and leave all the rest to him.[3]*

1. Fred W. Meuser, *Luther and the Preacher* (Minneapolis: Augsburg Press, 1983), p. 53.

2. Karl Barth, *Homiletics* (Westminster/John Knox Press, 1991), p. 104

3. Meuser, p. 58.

Chapter 1

✧✧✧✧✧✧✧

The Preacher's Edge[1]
(Written in narrative style)

The older I get, the more convinced I am that God created preaching as much for the benefit of the preacher as for what happens to the congregation. Could it be that in the divine scheme of things we have been equipping, instructing, and encouraging *ourselves* even more than those who sit at our feet when we preach? Could it be that this is what God intended all along? We go into our pulpits with zeal and a sense of mission to proclaim the gospel to our congregation, when all along, through God's spirit, God is inspiring *the preacher* with a sense of mission.

Several years ago when I was on sabbatical in Liberia, West Africa, there was a worship service at the Bong Mine parish conducted by missionaries Barry and Alice Lang from Canada. The public address system was rather antique, but the electricity was on at the moment. When it came time for Alice to lead a song about the power of God, she picked up the hand-held microphone so that she might be heard. On that damp, rainy morning, the microphone, which was not grounded, shorted against her moist lips. Barry told me that her hair stood on end, her eyes bugged out, and she shook all over. Those several hundred Liberians gathered there for worship were heard to say, "Dammy, Mama Lang! Dammy, dammy, dammy!"

I believe there is that kind of power available to us in our pulpits, also. I call it the preacher's edge.

Could it be that God had:

•The preacher of Ecclesiastes preach so he would gather the wisdom of religion, thus better equipping himself to teach the people?

9

•Noah preach righteousness in order to convince himself he was right about God when he seemed so alone?

•Peter preach at Pentecost to give himself a boost after the Ascension when Jesus was no longer physically with him?

•Paul preach so he might reinforce his own conversion to the Christian faith and overcome his own doubts?

•John the Baptist preach so that he might be convinced to repent, as well?

•Jesus the Christ preach in order to reassure himself that the kingdom was still very near?

•Barnabas preach in order to equip himself to do much needed peacemaking?

•Martin Luther, John Calvin, John Wesley preach so that they might remain strong in their call for reform at a time when they seemed so alone?

We have the privilege of power from the pulpit like all these saints of the church who experienced the preacher's edge. Perhaps the power is as close to us as it was to Alice Lang, but because we don't expect it, we really never hook up to it. Our hair doesn't stand on end, our eyes don't bug out, and we don't shake all over. And so, the change and charge that are possible never really happen to us or those to whom we preach.

Walter Brueggeman writes:

> *The task and possibility of preaching is to open out the good news of the Gospel with alternative modes of speech — speech that is dramatic, artistic, capable of inviting persons to join in another conversation, free of the reason of technique, unencumbered by ontologies that grow abstract, unembarrassed about concreteness. Such speech, when heard in freedom, assaults imagination and pushes out the presumed world in which most of us are trapped.[2]*

Before the Sermon

Just think what it means to us preachers that we preach week after week, Sunday after Sunday, in our congregations. Think what it means that we have to prepare for that sermon ahead of time. It

10

means we have the luxury of searching the scriptures and studying its implications for ourselves as well as for our people. It's part of our calling and we get paid for it as well! It certainly means we have the discipline weekly of distilling our faith into words understandable to us and our congregations and restating the glorious good gospel over and over again. It also means, at a regular time each week, we can give careful thought to our congregation's needs and refocus our ministry, as well as our own lives. Who else gets to do that kind of weekly evaluation and the renewal that comes from it?

In that preparation we certainly discover guidance for our own lives as we prepare to give advice to others. We learn how to deal with selfishness, greed, temptations, egomania, and the other real life, close-to-the-ground struggles. As we prepare to advise others, we gain insight on how we should behave.

You see, we have the luxury every week of quiet time, solitude, and rest from the hassle of daily ministry. It's almost like a spiritual retreat when we get to feed on the scripture and dialogue directly and anew with the Almighty.

As we prepare to preach, we are refreshed, refocused, and reminded of life's priorities. That ought to improve our parenting, our marriage, and our coping with loneliness as well.

And think how we are kept in tune with the life and presence of Christ if we follow the church year in our sermon preparation:
• The expectation and hope of Advent
• The wonder of Christmas
• The surprises of Epiphany
• The forgiveness of Lent
• The new life of Easter
• The inspiration and spirituality of Pentecost

As we go into that period of time called sermon preparation, we learn once more who we are and what our relationship to God, who called us to preach, can be. The others in our community view us as holy people who speak directly for and with God.

We also have the chance to reflect on our practice of ministry as we prepare to address all the lay ministers of the congregation and see that they are well-equipped to do the ministry they are called to do through their baptism. All this is in the preparation to preach. We haven't even gotten to the pulpit yet! Brueggemann quotes Walt Whitman from *Leaves of Grass:*

> *After the seas are all crossed, as they seem already crossed,*
> *after the great captains and engineers have accomplished their work,*
> *after the noble inventors, after the scientists, the chemists, the geologist, ethnologists,*
> *finally shall come the poet worthy of that name,*
> *the true Son of God shall come singing his songs.*[3]

During the Sermon

One of the major things that happens to us when we preach is what I call empathy transference. To me, it means love-making between preacher and congregation. Thoe people so want us to do well, and they love us and tell us that through their eyes and body language. This becomes a very intimate time with God and God's people where we are embraced and caressed by God and by God's people as we communicate back and forth, pulpit to pew and pew to pulpit. In that empathy transference, a bonding also takes place. It's good to know that we are loved and cared for and that's communicated to us as we preach. We feel revered and loved just as we are with all our imperfections and trepidations.

My mother always developed a nervous stomach whenever I would do public speaking as I was growing up. I think she still does when she is in the audience. I had similar feelings when my sons played football or my daughter performed on the harp. And when our youngest, Sarah, was the first girl to play boys' Little League in Richland County, Ohio, our entire family would sit on the bench to make sure that our "second base person" was treated well. And so when we preach, our congregational family empathizes with us like that.

We get a rush of inspiration and a sense of being in the special presence of the Almighty — and in these days of drugs and alcohol, that's a legitimate high!

One of the real surprises about preaching is that we will probably be better at it than humanly possible. I am sure of this!

We can actually be much better than our human skills, education, and experience would allow. That's the work of the holy spirit which surrounds us, lifts us up, and is *the preacher's edge*. In other words, we are lifted out of our human limitations to experience the thrill of God taking over and speaking through us. If that makes me a mystic, so be it. Fred Meuser claims:

> *Much is made of the doctrine of the real presence in Luther's sacramental theology. He also had another presence — the real presence of Christ in proclamation. When the proclamation about Christ is the biblical message of God's judgement and grace, not only is the preacher's word God's Word, but when the preacher speaks, God is really present in speaking. In the sermon one actually encounters God. That makes preaching — and hearing — a most dangerous business.*[4]

There is a second place and time when we have a bonus to our preaching that is simply unexplainable in terms of human communication. Not only is there that edge that causes the preacher to be better than he or she is capable, but there is also the edge in the hearer's interpretation of what is being said which is far better than what was preached! How else could one explain those comments at the door about the sermon which the preacher didn't realize he or she said . . . and may not have. For God's spirit enables each hearer to interpret the preached word through that individual's life experience, further boosting the significance of what the preacher had intended to say and giving him or her an edge.

There is also a time of affirmation and respect that gets us through the week. Like those who cheer in the stands for a football player to help get him through the second half, so too the congregation cheers for their pastor, helping him or her to get through the week.

There is enough fear about standing in front of this group that it gets the adrenaline moving and the heart pumping, giving our bodies the energy and strength we may not have thought we had. Any public speaker, singer, musician, or actor will tell you about that edge and the importance of getting it as they begin to perform.

13

A bonus is that we can be creative and experiment and risk and fail without fear of trying again the next week.

Yet another luxury of the pulpit in preaching is the catharsis of exploring frustrations. It's a good mental health technique for us to be able to release our anger and to experience the thrill of being frank and bold about ourselves. There is a form of group therapy that goes on when we preach to a congregation who knows us and whom we know.

The verbalization of our fear can also occur. In counseling it's called ventilation. Any preacher in touch with his or her congregation will work through and bring to the surface repressed material of his or her own. Whether that be done consciously or not, it's mighty healthy. Of course there is a danger of that taking over the sermon, but the fact that it is risky is also part of the value of doing it. Hence, preaching can benefit our own mental health. It can lift us out of depression as we work through problems and pump an exhilarating and fresh feeling into our own being, as well as the congregations'.

After the Sermon

Not unlike applause feeds the ego of a performer and gives encouragement to risk again, so the comments, greetings, and handshakes at the door give us immediate positive feedback. It's almost instant gratification. We gain larger doses of affirmation and expressions of love and caring than we really deserve. But it does help and that gives us strength to go out and do our best for these people of God again.

And we really have said things beyond our human capacity which now can be printed. Editors always advise those of us who publish our sermons never to compose the final draft until after preaching it. They evidently have learned that there is something extra which happens in the actual preaching of the sermon. They want us to capture God's contribution as our own profundity for the final product.

Our preaching adds to our own certainty of the gospel. Like someone who whistles in the dark and begins to own the behavior of being brave, so we preach with intensity and become even more

14

convinced of the good news we proclaim. And the more convinced we are, the better we convey the message. Our character has now changed because of what we have preached, so we become it and believe it. I remember a classmate at Wittenberg University who was a good actor and played the part of King Lear in a Shakespeare drama. He was a Stanislaus method actor who so became the character of King Lear that he never broke out of it the rest of his life! While that's a drawback to method acting, its advantage is that we can so preach in a way in the pulpit that it can become a part of who we are from then on.

Implications for Preaching

If you accept my premise so far of what happens to us when we preach, I'd like to continue by listing seven implications of preaching:

1. The process, including preparation and delivery, must be filled with prayer. We must learn how to open ourselves to God's spirit. That is, actually drench ourselves in God's presence until we are filled with the spiritual. That fullness spills over and inundates sermon notes and sermon proclamation.

2. We must expect great things to happen and thus allow for that edge of God's surprises in our preaching. After all, the real serendipity of preaching is the joy of it!

3. We have to be free from manuscripts in order to allow for God's contribution to the sermon content and for the eye contact with God's people to love and encourage us so that they can draw us out as the spirit wishes.

4. We must always compose our sermon notes and practice our proclamation, preaching to ourselves as well as to the congregation. And we must never publish our sermon in printed form until after preaching it so that the inspirational edge to the content can be made.

5. We must always practice out loud in the holy place where we preach to encourage the spirit to begin and continue the possible inspiration. (See chapter 14 on "Warming Up Message And Messenger.")

6. We must practice a certain reverence for the pulpit as a holy place where miracles happen in us when we allow them and the congregation encourages them.

7. We must not see the preparation to preach and preaching as grim duties, but as marvelous opportunities and edges in our ministry which deeply benefit us as well as our congregation.

No wonder God calls us to preach:

•Our people sit with us like my family did when Sarah was "second base person."

•We have great opportunity to work through our frustrations and ventilate our feelings.

•There is an empathy transference between us and the congregation.

•It's a wonderful luxury of retreat each week to prepare in God's presence.

•We have an edge which makes us far better than we really are.

So, like Luther, Jesus, John the Baptist, Paul, Peter, and Noah, we preach and we are changed because of it. Perhaps that's what God intended all along.

"Dammy, Mama Lang! Dammy, dammy, dammy!"

---

1. From Jerry Schmalenberger, *Plane Thoughts On Parish Ministry* (Lima, OH: CSS Publishing, 1994).

2. Walter Brueggemann, *Finally Comes The Poet* (Philadelphia: Fortress Press, 1989), p. 3.

3 From Walt Whitman's *Leaves Of Grass*, cited in Brueggemann, Preface (page not numbered).

4. Fred W. Meuser, *Luther, The Preacher* (Minneapolis: Augsburg, 1983), p. 13.

Chapter 2

❖❖❖❖❖❖❖

An Affirmation Of
Preacher And Preaching

Let us begin this work on preaching and preachers by examining the scripture for an affirmation of the task to which we have been called and the edge given us as we do it. Preaching has a very long history. In Ecclesiates 1:1 and 12 we read about the "one who addresses an assembly," that is, the preacher or the one who collects or gathers. People gathered together for instruction or wisdom that had been collected together for purposes of teaching. So there seems to be very early an office of "the preacher" or "the teacher."

There are other Old Testament preachers like:

•Noah, who preached righteousness (2 Peter 2:4-5).

•Jonah . . . "because they turned from their sins when they heard Jonah preach" (Matthew 12:41).

•Moses . . . "I am a poor speaker." "I will help you to speak and I will tell you what to say" (Exodus 4:10-16). So Moses is given a preaching partner who turned out to be his brother Aaron.

In the Book of Acts we read about Peter preaching to the people of Jerusalem on Pentecost and in Acts 3:15 the words: "We are witnesses to this." It seemed that basic to this apostolic style of preaching was "a witness to these things."

We read further about first century preaching in Acts 8:40 where Phillip is going from Azotus to Caesarea and "preached the good news in every town." In Acts 9:20 Paul preaches after his conversion that Jesus was "the son of God." According to that biblical account his preaching in the synagogues like Damascus became even more powerful. Paul and Barnabas and other apostles' sermons were called "a message about grace." In the fourteenth chapter of Acts there is a marvelous reference to Paul and Barnabas preaching the good news in Derby and winning disciples. Again, they preach in Perga according to Acts 14:25.

The objectives of these biblical characters in their preaching seemed to be winning converts and nourishing the faith.

There are a number of famous sermons in the Bible that ought to give us a lift in the task that we perform. In Acts 2, Peter's sermon on Pentecost, three thousand were baptized as a response to the message. We also have recorded in Acts 10 Peter's sermon at Caesarea when Peter used the narrative style of preaching and admits his own change of heart. In this sermon it's interesting to notice that it wasn't something new but rather the same old story told again and with conviction.

Saint Paul preached at Athens a dialogue sermon of sorts as we read in Acts 17. And Paul and Silas are preaching and teaching. Their content is recorded as being about Jesus and the Resurrection. It's interesting to note the use of contemporary and local settings and illustrations as they give their sermons. Paul, for instance, gave a sermon about an unknown god as he looked at a statue to one unknown there on Mars hill in Athens.

In the Book of Hebrews, Chapter 3, we find a relation between preacher and listener. In the twelfth verse notice that the approach is "my fellow believers" and in verse fourteen "all partners with Christ. . . ."

Perhaps the first preacher recorded in the New Testament was John the Baptist. In Luke 3, beginning at the third verse, we have a portion of his sermon with the focus "turn away from your sins and be baptized, and God will forgive your sins." Then he uses an Old Testament text. And crowds come out to hear him! It seems as though John the Baptist had four themes in his preaching: justice, repentance, good news, and the coming of Jesus.

Let us turn to Jesus as a preacher. In Matthew 4 John is in prison and Jesus begins to proclaim to the people that they should "turn from their sins" and that the "kingdom of Heaven is near."

Recorded in Luke 4 is Jesus' first sermon in his home church. Verse 21 illustrates how Jesus' sermon came alive when he claimed that the scripture was coming true that very day.

In Matthew 5 we read the Beatitudes which were probably Jesus' sermon themes that the disciples could remember later and write down. Notice how they use very common, everyday images: the poor, children, kingdom, salt, and light.

Matthew 13 tells how Jesus used parables and stories for his preaching. He was certainly the first narrative preacher. He took such things as soils, weeds, mustard seed, yeast, treasure, pearl, net, homeowner, that the people see every day and gave them special metaphorical meaning with the Gospel.

We have a grand affirmation from the scripture of our task as preachers. In Ephesians 4 we read how the preacher, like a teacher, was a person who had received a special gift and in verse 12 the preaching was done in order to build up the body of Christ. Notice that verse 15 tells us that preaching was "speaking the truth in a spirit of love."

The first chapter of First Corinthians says that preaching is to tell the good news in order to make sure that Christ's death on the cross is not robbed of its power. Verse 23 assures us we proclaim the crucified Christ when we preach. The second chapter begins explaining that God's secret truth is relayed through us. God's power is set free through our preaching. Not with big words or wisdom, but with convincing proof and the power of God's spirit.

In Colossians 1:23 we learn that hope was gained when the Gospel was proclaimed.

Titus 1 calls us chosen and sent folks who have hope of eternal life proclaimed to them.

According to the New Testament the Christian message in preaching is "the word." Acts 15 assures us that we have been chosen to preach the good news so that our hearers could hear and believe. Acts 17 talks about a word of truth that might be a bit more confrontational. Philippians 2:16 mentions the word of life when it says ". . . as you offer them the message of life." And Hebrews 5 says that preaching gives us the ability to distinguish between good and evil and reminds us that people of all statuses and degrees of sanctification hear our message. Some are like children yet on breast milk and others are like grown-ups on solid food.

I especially like Second Corinthians 5 when it talks about preaching as a word of reconciliation and making friends of God. This is a beautiful concept of our calling.

Acts 13 calls it a word of salvation: ". . . It is to us that this message of salvation has been sent." And First Corinthians 1:18 calls it preaching a word of the cross. God's power from the cross is delivered through the pulpits we occupy.

In *Finally Comes the Poet* Walter Brueggemann claims: "The Gospel is thus a truth widely held, but a truth greatly reduced. It is a truth that has been flattened, trivialized, and rendered inane. Partly, the Gospel is simply an old habit among us, neither valued or questioned."[1] He then concludes: "Poetic speech is the only proclamation worth doing in a situation of reductionism, the only proclamation, I submit, that is worthy of the name preaching . . . the preacher has an awesome opportunity to offer an evangelical world: an existence shaped by the news of the Gospel."[2]

All this is to say that if it has fallen on less than grand status and reputation we need to reclaim the place and power of the pulpit. It's obvious when we study the scripture that God has called us to a very special task of proclaiming this word to all those who will listen. Hans Van der Geest put it: ". . . preaching is a risk. In both good and not-so-good efforts we are dependent on the breath and spirit of God. It is a joy to know that."[3] We can take great satisfaction in being preachers and having the call to preach. The bonus of all this is that the preacher benefits most of all from the preaching. Read on, my friend, for ways that you might renew your preaching in the days ahead.

---

1. Walter Brueggemann, *Finally Comes The Poet* (Philadelphia: Fortress Press, 1989), p. 1.

2 *Ibid*, p. 3.

3. Hans Van der Geest, *Presence In The Pulpit* (John Knox Press, 1981), preface, v.

Chapter 3

Preaching For The Watch And Rewind Generation[1]
(Written in extended metaphor style)

Marina Gottschalk, a writer for the *Oakland Tribune*, told a fascinating story under the headline "Amnesty Program Triggers Recollection of Murder Plot." The city of Kensington, California, has been offering a gun amnesty program. A woman brought in a loaded pistol she said she bought 20 years ago to kill her husband! Gottschalk reported, "She never used the gun, but it presumably has been ready to go all these years."[2]

I have been loading a gun over the years of my preaching in the parish and teaching homiletics at Pacific Lutheran Theological Seminary as well. I'd like to fire off three shots across the bow of Christian congregations and preachers and see if that doesn't stimulate some radical new ways of thinking about our homiletical task. In doing so we can celebrate the edge that can be ours when we preach.

The three shots fired at preachers came from Ellen Goodman, Willie Nelson, and Thomas Long. Ellen Goodman has a syndicated newspaper column; Willie Nelson appears on *Hot Country Nights*; and Thomas Long provides bullets from a recent book on preaching called *The Witness of Preaching*.

The first shot comes from Ellen Goodman in her column titled "What Truly is Wrong with JFK?" As she talks about the fuss over Oliver Stone's movie *JFK*, she says these rather insightful words: "It is a fuss made by a generation that reads and writes for the minds of a generation that watches and rewinds."[3]

Our sermon consumers are used to VCRs and Super Nintendo — strong visual images — they watch and rewind. That certainly means for our preaching it is a different generation of people out

21

there listening. It has definite implications for what we say and how we say it.

Sermons must be short. Those who hear us now are used to television segments of twelve and half minutes at the most before a commercial. They simply do not have the discipline to concentrate for any longer than that.

Sermons must be earthy. They must talk about those things which so dominate our lives, like sex, money, lust, and love. During rating weeks on television we can get a good idea of what the media folks, through market research, have determined attracts viewers and listeners. David J. Burrell says:

> There are preachers who read beautiful essays on themes more or less closely related to theology and ethics; but that is not preaching. Talking about a thing is not preaching. The essayist takes his hearer by the hand and leads him round and round a center; the preacher takes his hearer by the hand and escorts him to the next town. It is thus that preaching helps men on.[4]

Because our people live in such high-pressure, tension-producing times, sermons need to be full of humor and contain the ingredient of the playfulness of God. For a generation who "watch and rewind," we also cannot assume such things as knowledge of the Bible stories or that they have been in attendance the week before — or ever. It has to be the whole gospel each time, fast forward speed and still-frame imagery.

Notice how in a television mini-series they catch you up with what has taken place previously before launching into this week's story. We must do the same with the gospel story.

Certainly for the "watch and rewind" generation we must pay more attention to our own physical appearance and use a lot more visual aids.

Variety is a must. It is important to vary the plot and use flashbacks, runs, and that which persuades, such as emotionally laden words, stereotypes, and verbal sanctions. These are the basic tools of persuasive speaking. Communication people have known this for a long time.

On occasion we ought to free ourselves from slavery to the church year or pericopes. For the person who is there for the first time or only attends a few times, it is probably not significant that it is Advent, Epiphany, or Lent. The preachers I now hear often spend more time justifying and explaining the season than they do in concentrating on the gospel! Sometimes the gospel of God is sacrificed and strained for the "propers" for the day.

I took a foster daughter to church recently. She had lived with us while going to college, then moved out to the West Coast. She hadn't been in church for years. Along with my eight-year-old grandson, we went to church. How hopeful I was that the gospel would shine through in enough completeness that she would be reminded of her heritage and that my grandson would hear that which he rarely hears in his home and never hears in church because he does not attend. Did it shine through? Answer, as if it was your congregation we attended that Sunday.

I believe that the "watch and rewind" generation wants to *feel* as well as *understand* the message. We Lutheran preachers are almost always correct in our proclamation, but not always interesting. That's Ellen Goodman for you. It's her ammunition and my first shot across the bow of us preachers. Later in her article she writes: "Those of us who are print people — writers and readers — are losing ground to the visual people — producers and viewers."[5] Perhaps we preachers need to become much better equipped as producers and viewers as we preach to the visual people.

Keep it Close to the Ground

The second shot I want to fire from a gun like that of the Kensington woman who kept hers loaded for twenty years is from Willie Nelson, the famed country western singer. He appeared recently, along with Loretta Lynn and Mickey Gilley, on an NBC Sunday night show, *Hot Country Nights*. Willie Nelson was introduced at the country music awards as the country musician who wrote and sang his music "close to the ground." That is my shot to you. Keep your sermon close to the ground!

23

In *Interactive Preaching,* D. Stephenson Bond writes

> *If we are to preach with insight, powerful language, and passion, we must learn to come down from the pulpit heights. The purpose of preaching has a new perspective from below rather than from above. Although the distance from the pulpit to the pew is only a matter of a few feet, those steps down from the chancel can be the most difficult journey a seminary trained minister ever has to undertake. The distance between the pulpit and the pew is the distance between a sermon about experience and a sermon experience; between a sermon about the Kingdom and a Kingdom encounter; between a sermon that describes in scholarly detail the various biblical and theological perspectives on transformation, and a sermon that is transformative.* [6]

Country music isn't my favorite, but I listen to see why it is so popular. It seems that when folk like Tammy Wynette and Willie Nelson sing, they sing about real life like heartbreak, divorce, death, kids disappointing parents, lovers leaving and cheating on each other, and revenge. They sing about loaded guns, like the one brought in to the Kensington police station.

Recently on the television show *Hot Country Nights,* Hank Williams, Jr., sang, "It ain't easy." The Grand Ole Opry has a segment called "Hurting Songs." This says a lot to me about our preaching. The theological words have to go! We must deal with the nitty-gritty issues of the day.

All this means that we will probably need to involve laity to help us keep our preaching close to the ground where they are and have need. It means we ought to keep a homiletical journal with us at all times, writing down those perceptions and insights that we observe as we live real life. This can be a great source of sermon material when we get ready to compose our proclamation. It also means we have to learn to share our own struggles and heartaches just like the country western singer does.

Preaching to human needs demands the ability to visualize the congregation, even while the sermon is being prepared . . . in a congregation of five hundred people, it is reasonable to assume that at least one hundred have been so recently bereaved as to feel an acute sense of loss. Probably a third of the married persons are facing problems of personality adjustment that may weaken or destroy their home life. At least one half of the five hundred can be assumed to have problems of emotional adjustment at school, work, home, or community that endanger their happiness. Others may have neuroses ranging from alcohol addiction to lesser forms of obsessions and anxiety states. Perhaps fifteen or more are homosexually inclined and another 25 depressed. Another hundred may be suffering from so great a feeling of guilt or fear of discovery that their peace of mind and health are jeopardized . . . here are the souls burdened with sin, fearful of life and death, injuring themselves by pride and jealousy, or making life miserable for others through resentments and masked hatred. Here are the souls who seek forgiveness, a faith to live by, an understanding of themselves to make their living more meaningful, and a basis for goodwill and sympathy to take the edge off their aggressiveness.[7]

A number of years ago when I was a pastor in Mansfield, Ohio, my wife hurried out of our home one Sunday morning, loaded all the kids in the station wagon, and being a bit late, drove at a rather high rate of speed down the hill toward the church. As they descended the hill, the kids heard a terrible screeching sound on the top of the car moving from the front windshield back to the rear window. By the time they got to the bottom of the hill, they could see our cat's tail hanging down behind that rear window. The cat had tried its best to hang on up there, digging its claws into the paint as best it could, but losing ground all the way!

It's the way many of us find ourselves in this lifestyle we try to live. Our sermons must take seriously this frantic life we are living and offer some help for surviving it.

Willie Nelson knows, Hank Williams, Jr., knows, and I think I understand now. I have been saving this "close to the ground" shot and the "watch and rewind shot" just as the woman did her pistol in Kensington. It calls for a new approach to visual people who want to hear the gospel applied to everyday life like theirs.

Preaching As Witness

Ammunition for my third shot comes from Thomas Long in his book, *The Witness of Preaching.* Long gives us three master metaphors for the preacher:

1. *The herald.* Like the Old Testament prophets, the courage has to be there to tell the truth. Long claims that heralds do not aspire to be artists, they aspire to be servants of the word. "Heralds come to the people with news from the king. Heralds provide the occasion for the hearing of the voice beyond the preacher's voice — the very word of the living God."[8]

2. *The pastor.* According to Long the crucial dimension of preaching is an event, something that happens inside the hearer when we see ourselves as pastor preachers. "Healing is often the point. The primary question is not what will I say, but what do I want to happen. Often preaching becomes basically a resource for human growth."[9]

3. *The story teller.* The story teller preacher actually puts the best of both the above images together. "We like stories, we live out our lives in stories, we remember in stories, we shape our values through stories. Sermons then have plots rather than points."[10] We know the beauty of the story teller preacher as he or she intersects his or her own story, the story of the individuals in the congregation and community, God's story of salvation, and the community's story of God's presence with them.

This third shot carries with it yet a fourth image which Long gives us in addition to those listed above.

4. *Preacher as witness.* I really like this concept that the preacher is basically a witness. It emphasizes for me the authority of the preacher in a new way. "Not rank and power, but because of what the preacher has seen and heard. Witnesses testify to events and to *the* event which is the encounter between God and ourselves."[11]

The implications for this shot of "preacher as witness" means that we are freed up to share our own experiences in the sermon and that we see the sermon in preaching *for the preacher* as well as for those who listen to it. The joy of it is that the more one witnesses to his/her faith, the more one believes, and the more one believes, the more one is able to witness. Think of that dynamic effect on the preacher!

Long says:

> *The herald just simply doesn't look carefully enough or take into account the community in which the sermon is delivered. The pastoral preacher is almost always too clinical and preaches to individuals with their individual problems, which rarely leads to a congregation seeing itself as a mission. The story teller image is worthwhile, but it's tempting to just concentrate on the narratives of the scripture.*[12]

So let's try to be witnesses in the pulpit. I like that idea. It's my third shot and comes right after Willie Nelson's "close to the ground" bullet and Ellen Goodman's "watch and rewind" bullet.

I don't know the name of that woman who turned in her loaded gun to the Kensington police (or that of her husband, who was in danger all those twenty years). But, like that woman, I too have saved up my shots. And it has been very rewarding to fire three of them off for present preachers concerning our preaching. If any have hit you, perhaps your congregation will rejoice and we can all reload! And read on . . . .

----

1. Jerry Schmalenberger, article in *Lutheran Partners* (July/August 1992).

2. Marina Gottschalk, "Amnesty Program Triggers Recollection of Murder Plot," *Oakland Tribune*, January 4, 1992: 1.

3. Ellen Goodman, syndicated columnist, "What Truly is Wrong with JFK," *Oakland Tribune*, January 5, 1992: 5.

4. David J. Burrell quoted in: M. Reu, *Homiletics* (Chicago: Wartburg Publishing House, 1924), p. 124.

5. Goodman, *op. cit.*

6. D. Stephenson Bond, *Interactive Preaching* (St. Louis: CPB Press, 1991) pp. 4-5.

7. Edgar N. Jackson, *How to Preach to People's Needs* (Nashville: Abingdon Press, 1976), pp. 13 & 15.

8. Thomas G. Long, *The Witness of Preaching* (Louisville: Westminster/John Knox Press, 1989), pp. 25 and 27.

9. *Ibid.*, p. 32.

10. *Ibid.*, p. 37.

11. *Ibid.*, p. 44.

12. *Ibid.*, pp. 29, 33, and 40.

❖❖❖❖❖❖❖

Self-Care Of The Preacher
(Written in an extended metaphor style)

We were driving down Interstate 80 somewhere between the Sierra pass and Oakland, California. We overtook a big eighteen wheeler low boy truck with a very large earth moving machine it was transporting. A large sign on the rear of the low boy warned us "wide load."

After we proceeded about a half mile past the low boy we came upon a Chevrolet Impala that obviously was the lead car for the convoy. It also had big signs on it, "wide load." In addition, on the back bumper, was an aerial that went extraordinarily high into the air. Inside in the driver's seat was a man who was talking on a CB radio. Evidently he was driving along that freeway testing the underpasses to see if clearance was enough for the low boy transporting the earth moving machine. If the aerial would hit the overpass, it would set off an alarm in the Chevrolet and the driver would radio back to the driver of the truck. He would tell the driver to get his load centered in the middle of the freeway so that there would be clearance for what he was carrying.

I'd like to propose for you in this chapter some clearances we need to check out and suggest some indications that you as a preacher could be a bit off center and may not be fully benefiting from the edge you need to get centered again. It's probably an indication that the world has closed in on you and your ministry and heaven might be a little out of sight. We all have those times in our ministry when preaching becomes almost a drudgery and if the following symptoms are yours, let the alarm go off and consider the remedies that can get you centered again on your way of proclamation of the gospel. There's no doubt about it, if we keep ourselves centered in the preaching task we can move mountains.

When we begin to put off getting started in preparing the sermon, it is one of the strong signals that we have allowed ourselves to become off center in our preaching. In the parish ministry it's always easy to rationalize that we have more pressing things to do in any day. At the same time, we may be feeling an anxiety and a sort of nagging in the belly which becomes a silent dread as we know Sunday is approaching and need to have a sermon prepared. Still, we put off starting work on it.

The alarm ought to go off and the lead car ought to be radioing back to the driver of the eighteen wheeler when we start to use the church's liturgy and other worship exercises to fill the preaching time. In many denominations' books of worship there are often the long version and the short version of whatever we do. If we put everything into the liturgy and worship service that's in that book, we can narrow down the preaching time to just a few minutes. That's tempting when we've lost a bit of our confidence that what we have to say is important. At the same time, if this is going on in our lives it probably will be communicated to the congregation that the sermon is no longer the climax or highlight of worship and it is just rather incidental that we have to preach at all.

Changing the name of the sermon to a homily or a message or even a sermonette is another signal that we might be off center on our preaching journey. I know one Lutheran Bishop who claims that when it's called a sermonette it probably means it's given short shrift. If this is the case, the antenna will probably be striking the top of the overpass and we'll be getting the message that something needs to be done to get centered on the preaching highway again.

When all humor and playfulness disappears from the content of our sermons it probably means preparation has become too much of a drudgery. Our Lord told wonderful human stories with an edge to them and we want always to do the same. If we begin to take on a holy tone or what we might call a "stained-glass voice," it's indicative that we have drifted from the center of our task.

One young lad growing up on a farm had just caught a rat and killed it and was bringing it in by the tail to show his mother. She was seated in the parlor of the farmhouse visiting with the pastor. The little boy came to the door of the parlor, not seeing the preacher, and exclaimed: "Mother, mother, I just caught this rat by the tail and then I stamped on it with my feet and . . . ." Then noticing that the preacher was there and listening, he added in a holy tone, ". . . God called it home!"

A sure sign that we have gotten off center on our preaching trip is heavy use of illustrations from sermon illustration books. Our sermon is stuffed full with stories about Alexander the Great, Abraham Lincoln, and Joan of Arc. If whole paragraphs are lifted from the *Interpreter's Bible*, William Barclay's *Daily Study Bible*, and various sermon services we've subscribed to, it's an indication that we need to make some real adjustments.

This ought to cause the alarm to sound too: when we begin to believe we can get by with old sermons or we can write sermons which can be used any time and any place and which are so general they'll do the task without any specifics. There's a wonderful story about Saint Paul preaching at Troas with a young man sitting in the window listening. The scripture claims Paul went on and on until the young man fell asleep and fell out of the window. While it's comforting to know that even Saint Paul bored people with the length and content of his preaching, we must preach in a style that is so relevant and exciting and close to the ground that it will be extremely interesting to those who hear.

Reading the gospel out loud for the first time in the actual worship service is another low clearance sign. The same can be said for delivering the sermon. If we are walking into the pulpit and giving it aloud for the first time when our parishioners are there to hear it, there's something basically wrong about our motivation and method of sermon preparation and delivery.

The danger lights ought to flash on the lead car if our sermon content omits speaking to the preacher and simply addresses "you people" in what it has to say about the gospel. If the sermon is not calling for changes in the preacher's life as well as the lives of the congregation, it needs to be re-examined and centered again.

It's a sure indication that there is a low overpass ahead when we start inviting all the visiting preachers we can. There are many ways we can duck the responsibility of preaching, like pulpit exchanges with other clergy, representatives of church institutions and agencies, and youth Sundays. Of course, we want to do some of these things but it is tempting to fill our pulpit with other people so that we don't have the responsibility of preparing and delivering the sermon. If that's happening to you, read on.

There are some preachers, in fact, who arrange to go to as many conferences and meetings of the church as possible and time it so they are gone on the weekend and someone else must do the preaching. This is an indication something's wrong. When we preachers use too many audio-visuals in place of the sermon, or cancel services often because of conditions like cold, snow, ice, and other "acts of God," it's a good indication that we need to make some real adjustments just like the driver of the eighteen wheeler in order to bring on the equipment that can move mountains right from the pulpit.

There's probably low clearance and danger indicated if we start to develop toward the end of the week some physical symptoms such as diarrhea, depression, sleeplessness, irritability, pain somewhere in our body, headaches, asthma attacks, trouble with colds, sinuses, and sore throats which affect the delivery of the sermon. These might be psychological as well as physical. We need to keep a close check on them, as they may indicate a certain dread that we need to overcome about our preaching.

When sermonizing becomes increasingly abstract and deals with issues without reference to our faith or seems rather belabored and dull, it's probably another indication that something is off center.

All the above signals which our preaching "antenna" might pick up can be brought about by other and more legitimate reasons, but putting several together probably indicates that we have a problem which needs to be addressed.

I'm hoping that by reading the following suggestion from a lead car, we might hear the driver announce in CB lingo: "Put the pedal to the metal, good buddy, and let her go to double nickel."

To help with getting your preaching task centered again and providing new excitement and motivation for sermon preparation and delivery, I would like to suggest the following possibilities:

32

1. Consider establishing a system of preaching partners who will help you prepare the sermon. I have explained this in much more detail beginning on page 110 of this book. It is a wonderful way to establish a solid partnership with the laity of the congregation, encourage good sermon listeners, and make it outright fun to prepare the sermon.

2. Take good note of your own spiritual health. It is extremely important that we preachers preach out of an overflow of our own spiritual experience. This means that we need to intentionally develop a daily routine to maintain our spirituality.

3. Physical health is also important. Preachers are athletes in the pulpit. We ought to appear healthy and robust, enthusiastic and inspired as we deliver the sermon. Have an annual physical check-up and know that your health is in peak condition so that you might preach well. Just as the athlete must train for playing the game, so the preacher must be in the same good physical condition to do the preaching.

4. In order that our health be the best possible so that the sermon is delivered as effectively as possible, schedule time for relaxation, time to play, time for good physical exercise. It could be that a stationary bicycle, jogging, running, walking and isometrics are just what's called for to improve our physical condition in the pulpit.

5. We have to have enough leisure time to muse and question and observe life around us.

6. As recommended on page 109, #8 in this book, there is just no substitute for keeping a good homiletical journal in which we note things that we observe, question, and muse over. Stories which you hear that have a punch can be noted with the punchline. Catchy phrases that you hear and can use in preaching may be written down. Articles from the local newspaper and stories from television and advertisements are always good. A couple of examples might be in order: the day I dictated this chapter I read in the Kingston, Jamaica, newspaper an article about a "side-man" who works on each public bus. There was a picture of one on the top of the bus putting luggage in place from its passengers. Evidently the side-man is responsible for the outside of the bus, people hanging out

of the windows and doors, and whatever luggage there might be. He takes care of the passengers. I had noted earlier in my journal about a side-man who stands close to and supports a soloist in a band. Now we might put those two together and come up with a wonderful metaphor that can serve as a vehicle for a sermon.

The very metaphor that I have extended about the lead car and the eighteen wheeler transporting earth moving machinery was observed and noted in my homiletical journal several years ago, waiting for just the right time to use it.

Another example of an entry in a homiletical journal comes from watching a D-Day special on CBS featuring Dan Rather and Norman Schwarzkopf. Schwarzkopf told how the paratroopers who were dropped at night behind the enemy lines were given little metal crickets to use in identifying each other in the dark so they could discover whether the person they heard in the dark was friend or enemy. Just think how that could be used in a close to the ground sermon some day!

7. There is also a great deal of strength, motivation, and inspiration for preaching in fellowship with other preachers. If there is a study group in your community on the pericopes, do your best to be a part of it. If there isn't one, perhaps you can be the person to start one.

8. There is a national organization called the Academy of Preachers. It is organized out of the Lutheran Theological Seminary at Philadelphia with chapters at Gettysburg, Pennsylvania; St. Paul, Minnesota; Berkeley, California; and Florida. This group is determined to see that the art of preaching is not lost and the respect for preaching and preacher is reclaimed. They want to recover the sermon as God's effective tool and learn from each other in doing so. It is their goal to develop a sense of self-worth as well as the craft of sermon construction and delivery. They also promise to pray for each other.

Well, there we were on Interstate 80. First overtaking a large eighteen wheeler on which an earth moving machine was mounted, we passed a Chevy Impala with warning lights and signs of "wide load." That aerial extended into the air to test out the height of the overpasses. The driver of the Impala radioed back the warnings and admonition to the eighteen wheeler to get centered. Perhaps we have given some indications that you might be drifting a bit off center and need to be pulled back where the clearance is best, the gospel is proclaimed, and mountains are moved because of it. It is my hope that this book will be one of the instruments through which you can celebrate a centeredness to your task and reclaim the preacher's edge. Saint Paul, in giving advice to young Timothy on his ministry, said, "Do your best to present yourself to God as one approved, a workman who does not need to be ashamed and who correctly handles the word of truth" (2 Timothy 2:15).

Chapter 5

✧✧✧✧✧✧✧

Pulpit Therapy

There is a quiet revolution going on right now in counseling therapy. The new technique is called "the narrative method," and it represents a radical paradigm shift in the therapeutic world. It can not only explain why narrative preaching gives us an edge but also can give us a number of new insights on sermon content, organization, and follow-through for our preaching.

In a recent "Lifestyle" article in *Newsweek* magazine, Goeffry Cowley and Karen Springen write, ". . . a small but growing number of psychotherapists are shedding ideas that have dominated their field for a century. The new approach is still far from orthodox, it's a fundamentally new direction in the therapeutic world named narrative therapy. At the heart of the new approach is the post-modernist idea that we don't so much perceive the world as interpret it."[1]

For narrative preachers the new counseling therapy is a description of why narrative preaching is so transforming for our congregational members and for the preachers themselves.

According to Michael White, an Australian therapist who seems to be the father of the movement, "No problem or diagnosis ever captures the whole of a person's experience. The person has other ways of acting and thinking, but they get neglected because they lie in the shadow of the dominant story."[2]

Four elements tend to dominate the narrative therapist's technique. First the therapist invites the client to *personify the problem*. Second the narrative therapist thinks of *personal identity as a story* that can be retold and redeemed.

The third element is unlike most approaches. Narrative therapy isn't a secretive transaction between the therapist and the client; the *community is engaged* in the renegotiation of identity.

37

The fourth element is called *extending the conversation*. Here the therapist writes a letter summing up the learnings of the therapy session and sends it to the counselee. These are called narrative letters. David Nyland writes: "Narrative letters enable me to have maximum impact in the least number of sessions."[3]

Help for Preachers

Preachers can learn a lot from these new insights into quality counseling. Over the years we have so fought "like the devil" against any personification of evil and sin that our congregants will be surprised when we identify those things that are eating away at our quality of life and discipleship and give them names and effective ways they pollute our existence. Sin, devil, evil, greed, culture, selfishness, addiction, guilt are all names for outward forces that attack us. The Scripture has a great deal to say about them and about how we can overcome them. Our sermons need to be filled with this empowerment to name those forces that are eating away at us and provide ways to overcome them. Bill O'Hanlon writes in the November/December issue of *Networker*, ". . . narrative therapists are able to acknowledge the power of labels while both avoiding the trap of reinforcing people's attachment to them and letting them escape responsibility for their behavior."[4]

The narrative therapist helps the client rework and retell his/her life story including the small victories and triumphs as well as the defeats. When we tell the biblical stories and stories of the saints, we can help the sermon listeners formulate their own stories as they hear the preachers and those recorded in history and the Bible. "This work is not about people discovering their 'true' nature, their 'real' voice," says White, "but about opening up possibilities for people to become other than who they are."[5]

We have that empowerment in the Christian faith to help people "become other than who they are" and have many stories in the Scripture of the presence of Christ actually helping it to happen.

Perhaps the newest and boldest idea in narrative therapy is the use of "extending the conversation." It has a great deal to say to us about sermon follow-up. The therapist writes a letter and summarizes the insights gained in the counseling session which is mailed to the client. "A client can hold a letter in hand, reading and rereading it days, months and years after the session."[6]

This throws a radical new light on how we interpret the letters of the Bible, Paul's epistles in particular, in our preaching. It is a different and new approach. Perhaps Paul wrote the follow-up letter after struggling with young Christians and provided for us nearly 2,000 years later something that we could read and gain insight from.

Certainly our sermon can be extended by offering such things as discussion groups about the sermon content, printed sermons available after the sermon is delivered, sermon summaries printed in the bulletin, feedback groups that help prepare and then evaluate the sermon, lay people who take part in discussion groups about what has been proclaimed.

Practical Applications

There are some very practical implications to this new idea of narrative method of therapy. It has certain implications for the content of what we preach. Let's be bolder again about naming not only sin in general, but the *sins* which are the results of the general *sin*. Let's talk from the pulpit about a seduction that goes on by the power which works against God. And instead of beating shame and guilt further into our sermon listeners, let's give them a way out by telling the gospel story and what Christ has done for us in particular in order that we can overcome the demonic seduction. The overarching emphasis ought to be on the power that God gives to get through.

Our sermon content certainly must include the many stories of the Bible and how these folks overcame their struggles. We ought also to be unafraid to tell our own story and the struggles, victories, and defeats we have experienced. Certainly the promise God gives that we have an Emmanuel (God With Us) needs to be told again and again as we formulate what it has been like to live with that Emmanuel equipment.

We ought to talk again about conversion. Narrative therapy simply identifies the fact that we do have considerable control over our lives and that we can change who we are and how we are. We

Christians can add: "with God's help." We do have a spirit that is available to us to bring about dramatic conversion and that ought to be named and invoked in the pulpit.

A Sample Sermon Outline

The following is a possible outline of a sermon plot and moves using the narrative method which is demonstrated in this new therapy:

1. Tell a story. It could be of one of the saints, the biblical heroes or heroines, a reformer, a religious hymn writer.

•Identify the external sins that attacked this person in his or her life story.

•Point out how he or she overcame these attacks.

•Read the Scripture and relate how we can use its advice and inspiration to empower ourselves to overcome as well.

2. Tell your own story as the preacher.

•Identify the external forces in your own life and how they influenced you.

•Point out how your faith took you through.

3. Now draw some insights:

•We all have external forces causing us pain.

•We all have a life story and may have forgotten the hopeful parts of it and the promises we have as Christians.

•We all have a communion of believers to help us through.

4. Ask the individual listeners to the sermon what their story might be.

•Ask them to identify what powers are trying to spoil their lives.

•Give some hope and encouragement because of the gospel's story of what Christ has done for us.

5. Tell your listeners that the body of believers (congregation) is part of our story.

•We can help each other bring Christ's presence to us.

•We can remind each other of the promises of Christ.

•We can affirm our strength to help us fight the outside powers.

Complete the narrative sermon by returning to the end of the story with which you began the sermon.

Empowering the Congregation

I believe this kind of preaching can empower the congregation to minister to each other and take seriously our theology of the ministry of all the baptized. Congregants are pointed to the sacraments, worship, rites, and the fellowship of believers as strengthening ways to help overcome those sins that attack us. The congregation can see itself as a support group for people who struggle with all the things that culture puts upon us during our lifetime.

There's also a therapy going on for the one who preaches the sermon! God has instituted preaching for the preacher's help as well as the congregation's. Formulating and telling our own story and the stories of Scripture certainly shape and redeem the preacher's story as well.

It's also possible for the preacher to externalize the congregation's problems and be reminded of its strength and its good times rather than just those times which are a struggle and problematic. This will help continue the ministry that is often hard work and can bring healing to the pastor as the people of God struggle to be faithful in their common ministries.

There's also a congregational therapy that must take place when we preach using the narrative method. The congregation hears the sermon and puts the preacher's faults outside the preacher onto a culture and world that is sin-filled and attacking from every side. It can also give a new view of the congregation and the task of the congregation to support a clergy who is preaching. The congregation hears a story they can identify with in the sermon and thus they redeem the congregation's history no matter how dismal it may have been from time to time. If this works well it can free the congregation of guilt for its poor track record and even convert a congregation from passivity to mission mindedness.

Berkeley, California, based therapists Jennifer Freeman and Dean Lobovits have written, ". . . a problem saturated dominant story tends to filter problem free experiences from a person's memories and perceptions, so that threads of hope, resourcefulness and capability are excluded from a person's description of self."[7]

41

We have a remedy for that in the preaching of the Gospel in narrative style. As Cowley and Springen described it in "Lifestyle," "Instead of looking for flaws in people's psyches, narrative therapy works at nurturing their forgotten strengths."[8] You and I who are preachers have many forgotten strengths to proclaim.

1. Geoffrey Cowley & Karen Springen, "Rewriting Life Stories," "Lifestyle," *Newsweek*, (April 17, 1995), p. 70.

2. "Rewriting Life Stories," p. 70.

3. David Nyland & John Thomas, "The Economics of Narrative," *Networker*, (Nov/Dec, 1994), p. 39.

4. Bill O'Hanlon, "The Promise of Narrative," "The Third Wave," *Networker*, (Nov/Dec, 1994), p. 24.

5. Mary Sykes Wylie, "The Promise of Narrative," "Panning for Gold," *Networker*, (Nov/Dec, 1994), p. 44.

6 David Epston, "The Promise of Narrative," "Extending the Conversation," *Networker*, (Nov/Dec, 1994), p. 31.

7. "Rewriting Life Stories," p. 70.

8. "Rewriting Life Stories," p. 70.

Transition

❖❖❖❖❖❖❖

As we move from the preacher to the sermon, consider Donald T. Campbell's list of potential sources of error on the part of the listener:

1. There is a good possibility that the average congregant will tend to shorten, simplify, and eliminate details from the message of the preacher. The longer the sermon, the greater the leakage.

2. The central section of the sermon is the least likely to be remembered.

3. A listening congregant is likely to omit detail and round off the remarks to obtain a general idea of what the preacher is saying.

4. People tend to interpret messages on the basis of their past experiences. If a preacher's past sermons have been uniformly ambiguous and uninspiring, new ones will be decoded in a similar manner.

5. Congregants are likely to modify a new sermon to sound like previous messages — "we have heard all this stuff before" — which may be far from the truth.

6. In general, the listener will qualify remarks or sermons so that they conform to the listener's prior expectations.

7. The listening congregant tends to alter messages so that they are in closer harmony with the listener's own viewpoints and attitudes.

8. It is quite natural for persons to listen to a sermon or a conversation in evaluative terms. However, many listeners judge messages merely as positive or negative, brilliant or stupid.

9. When listening to a sermon with a group, persons tend to distort the message to conform to others' interpretations. Being part of a group often causes filtered message reception, or "groupthink." [1]

Keep in mind these warnings as we now take up the construction of the sermon based on audience reaction.

1. Donald T. Campbell, "Systemic Error in the Part of Human Links in Communication Systems," cited in Myron R. Chartier, *Preaching as Communication*, Abingdon Preacher's Library, ed. William D. Thompson (Nashville: Abingdon, 1981), pp. 52-53.

Chapter 6

❖❖❖❖❖❖❖

Sermon Moves According To Listener Reaction

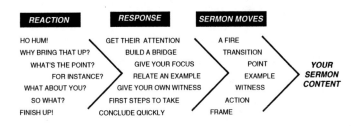

Sermon Structure From Congregational Reaction

Down through the years, those who have given effective speeches have done so because they followed an old and simple formula based on audience reaction. It can give us our edge in preaching today. Already in 1935 Richard C. Borden was explaining the listener's laws for speech organization with a formula of how the audience felt and the steps the speaker should take to cope with those feelings. He claimed, "It is so simple that you can write it on your thumbnail:

1. Ho hum!
2. Why bring that up?
3. For instance!
4. So what?"[1]

In order to meet these four stages of audience reaction Borden recommended the following four-step organization of a speech:

1. Start a fire — kindling a quick flame of spontaneous interest right away.

2. Build a bridge — between listener's island of own interest to the heart of the message.

3. Get down to cases — giving purposive assertion about the subject.

4. Ask for action — answering the listener's question: So what?

In the above speech theory for persuasive speaking, often referred to as "the magic formula for persuasive speaking," we can look first at the congregant's reaction to the preaching time and then move to recommending a formula for organizing a sermon.

We can modify and expand the formula thus: Listener's Reaction to the Sermon.

1. Ho Hum — settle in, yawn, shift mind into neutral.

2. Why bring that up? — Interesting, but what does that have to do with me?

3. What's the point? — Give me the heart of it.

4. For instance — I see, now an example to be sure I understand.

5. What about you? — I wonder what the preacher believes?

6. So what? — I'm convinced. What should I do now?

7. Finish up — Let's get out of here and get started.

If you believe that pretty well describes how the listeners respond during the preaching time, then the following can serve as the major moves in a sermon that takes seriously the listener's listening habits:

1. Get the attention of the listeners right away.

2. Build a bridge with one foundation on the hearers present and one on the truth to be communicated.

Bridge

Present Situation   Gospel Focus

3. Give the point of the message.

4. Give an example of the truth communicated.

5. Tell your own witness to the Gospel.

6. Give the first action steps to be taken because of this truth.

7. Frame it. Close by bringing the listener back to the fire where you started.

Let's now take each of these sermon moves and see their implications in our sermon construction.

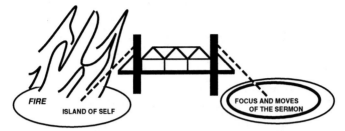

FIRE

ISLAND OF SELF

FOCUS AND MOVES OF THE SERMON

THE FIRST THREE MOVES OF AN AUDIENCE REACTION SERMON

1. *Start a fire* — kindling a quick flame of spontaneous interest right away. This is in reaction to the "ho hum" and settling in that takes place after the first part of the worship service and when the preaching time has arrived. We need to work long and hard on that first sentence! It ought not be mish-mash or holy words or pronouncements even on the text. We should read the scripture outside the pulpit and then move into the pulpit. The first thing out of our mouth ought to be this fire which gets attention. Save the prayer for the end or at the altar.

Alan H. Monroe lists nine factors of attention which are believed to be capable of capturing the spontaneous attention of an audience:

1. Activity or movement	4. Familiarity	7. Conflict
2. Reality	5. Novelty	8. Humor
3. Proximity	6. Suspense	9. The Vital

People are most interested in what concerns them personally. We are concerned most with something that affects us personally. That always gets our attention.[2]

Construct a bold sentence which is attention-getting and almost shocking. Eugene Lowry in his book *The Homiletical Plot* calls this "upsetting the equilibrium." Sometimes a story that is attractive will work to build this fire. Often the best way to use a story in this situation is to start in the middle of the story much like many of the television programs do. Lowry writes: "The first step in the presented sermon, then, is to upset the equilibrium of the listeners, and is analogous to the opening scene of a play or movie in which some kind of conflict or tension is introduced."[3]

Sometimes a news event will work here. The first line in a newspaper story is almost always written to build a fire. When you go into the pulpit do not picture your listeners as all ears and ready to hear every word you have to say. Build a fire for attention.

Some don'ts: "The lesson for today tells us . . . ". "When I sat down to write this sermon . . . ."

A couple do's: "According to the Associated Press, ninety-some passengers on a ferry boat off the coast of Finland drowned in the sea last Tuesday. Where was God?"

Another example: "As teenagers we would find 'dummy Parker' in the public restroom and taunt him until he ran and hid from us."

2. Now that the fire is built and we have our listeners' attention, it's time to *build a bridge*.

$$\text{Present Situation} \nearrow \text{Bridge} \searrow \text{Gospel Focus}$$

The success of the sermon hangs on how well we bridge from what we used to get attention to the main focus of the sermon. Our people live on an island of their little world so we must bridge them over to the Gospel or, using Luther's analogy of the two kingdoms, we build a bridge from the kingdom of the world to the kingdom of God.

The bridge ought to answer the listener's question, "Why bring that up?" It will assure those whose attention you now have that they have an important reason(s) for listening further.

An example: "We all have questioned whether a far-off God even cares when disaster like the sinking of that ferry boat takes place. We almost say out loud — why did God allow that horrible event to happen if God is a God who loves us?"

Or a second example: "How we treat those who don't conform to our notion of what's normal is something we all need to think through. Perhaps you aren't especially proud of the way you have treated society's disenfranchised and deviant from all the rest of us."

We only internalize what we are convinced we need to learn. The bridge shows our listeners what they need to know.

Regardless of our subject, we must first get the listeners' attention and then convince them that it is crucial for them to consider what's coming next from the Gospel.

3. It's now time to *announce our focus*. It ought to answer briefly and clearly the point of the sermon. Some would advocate putting the scripture text here. I would prefer not. This is a place to state a crisp, positive sentence that could stand alone and be remembered. It ought to be short enough that it can be repeated throughout the remainder of the sermon.

An example: "The point is, there is a big difference between what God wants to happen to us and what God allows to happen to us. Because there is a disaster doesn't mean God is absent."

Or another example: "Jesus modeled a life of love for the unlovely. He wants us to love them also."

4. *Relate an example*. Our listeners are listening, are sure this applies to them, have the point of the message, and now they are asking to be given a "for instance." And so we relate an example or examples.

The example is where and when we can cite the scripture that throws light on the focus of the message. It is the text for the day which led us to construct the first part of the sermon the way we did. Notice that we begin with the scripture as we prepare the sermon but save it to this point in order for it to have the most impact on the message.

If it is an extended metaphor sermon, it would be the main body of the narrative with which we built the fire in the first place. In other sermons it would be one or several scriptural references from which we have obtained the main point.

Place here several examples, alternating them from the scriptural example and contemporary society's examples. Throughout the giving of these examples repeat over and over the words of the point.

An example: "Consider the story Jesus told of the man beaten in the ditch along the road to Jericho."

5. The listeners are now wondering about what the preacher believes. Here is the place to *give our own witness*.

Since most preachers have been schooled in seminaries which told them never to mention themselves in the sermon, and since many of us are very shy about personal witness, this can feel awkward at first, but can be the most compelling portion of the sermon.

In his book, *The "I" of the Sermon*, Richard Thulin makes the case well for giving one's own witness.

> *I have claimed that the preacher's personal story lies at the heart of the pulpit presence of the "I." Whether that presence appears in the form of declaration, or in the assumption of responsibility, or in the surrender of oneself to the content and dynamics of the sermon, it must locate its identity in personal story. Preachers, I have suggested, will not even know what they are talking about unless what they say is consciously anchored in their own stories.[4]*

> *In preaching, as in other forms of pastoral ministry, the preacher cannot hide. People demand a clear and honest word from the one who speaks. That demand will not be met by a barrage of Bible verses or by a host of brilliant quotations from recognized theologians. That demand will be met only when the preacher speaks the truth out of his or her own life.[5]*

Simply state what you believe about the point of the sermon and/or how this idea impacts your life.

An example: "When my father died I had a terrible time believing God was there for me or that God even cared that my father died and I lost him. Then my pastor explained the difference between what God permits to happen and what God causes to happen. He said God didn't want me to lose my father but simply had to allow natural law to operate. I was relieved and grateful."

Or another example: "Like teasing dummy Parker as a teenager, I still am repulsed by those who are too deviant from the normal. I continually have to be reminded that they also are God's people — and if for no other reason I must love them on God's behalf."

6. *First steps to take.* After so much motivation and inspiration has been spoken in the sermon, it's natural that the listener is asking "so what?" Here is where so much of our preaching is weak. We fail to instruct the congregation on what they should do individually and together because of the message they have just heard proclaimed from the pulpit. Notice in that second chapter of Acts

how Peter preached his Great Sermon on Pentecost and the people responded by asking him what they should do about it. Peter told them to repent and be baptized. And they did! So we must provide the possible steps to take in the listeners' lives and ministry as they leave the worship service and return to the real world of work, life and play.

An example: "During the altar prayer today let's pray for the victims of that horrible disaster off the coast of Finland. Let's pray for the survivors, too, that they can understand the difference between what God permits to happen and what God causes to happen. Try seeking out people in our community who have suffered great loss and find a way to minister to them, explaining the difference between what God permits and what God causes to happen."

Or another instance: "As a congregation, let's get a shelter for battered women established in our town. Our church council ought to be challenged to provide the space here in our building. Perhaps this week you could seek out a person our community has not treated well — maybe even people you don't think deserve it — and do some nice thing for them."

7. *Frame it.* Just as soon as we begin to give specific steps, the normal thing for the listener's mind is to think about doing those things and desiring the sermon to end. So we conclude by framing it.

Framing a sermon means to end it by returning to the first few sentences with which we began the sermon. This communicates that we have prepared carefully and that we have completed that which we set out to do.

An example: "When we think about those (980) passengers dying in the dark of night off the coast of Finland it's a terrible thought. We can be certain, however, that God was there with them and God's heart aches for their survivors as well."

A second illustration: "My prayer is that God will forgive me for those times when I joined other teenagers in my town to taunt dummy Parker there in the public restroom. Now I'm confident that he also was one of God's people and Christ has taught me to love the 'dummy Parkers' of the world on God's behalf."

51

owe is critical of sermons because:

Sermons often contain too many ideas.
Sermons have too much analysis and too little answer.
Sermons are too formal and impersonal.
4. *Preachers assume that lay people have a greater knowledge and understanding of biblical and theological lore and language than they actually do.*
5. *Sermons are too propositional; they contain too few illustrations; and the illustrations are often too literary and not helpful.*[6]

You can see that we have in the old magic formula for persuasive speaking a technique for overcoming these criticisms and proclaiming the good Gospel to our people but ordering it in such a fashion that it answers the listeners' questions as they come out throughout the preaching. This formula can move us from preaching correct sermons with which no one can debate to preaching sermons which are interesting, inviting, and which move congregation and individuals to specific action.

It is the assurance of John McClure also when he writes: "A rhetorical schema for preaching is meant to help the preacher organize the diverse verbal components of preaching so that they can be strategically or purposely effective for a particular congregation."[7]

---

1. Borden, *Public Speaking — As Listeners Like It!* (New York and London: Harper Brothers, 1935), p. 3

2. Batsell Barrett Baxter, *Speaking For The Master* (New York: Macmillan Company, 1954), p. 111.

3. Eugene Lowry, *The Homiletical Plot* (Atlanta: John Knox Press, 1980), pp. 30-31.

4. Richard L. Thulin, *The "I" of the Sermon* (Philadelphia: Fortress Press, 1986), p. 24.

5. *Ibid.*, p. 13.

6. Reuel L. Howe, *Partners in Preaching* (New York: Seabury Press, 1967), pp. 26-31.

7. John S. McClure, *The Four Codes of Preaching* (Minneapolis: Augsburg Fortress, 1991), p. 3.

Chapter 7

❖❖❖❖❖❖❖

The Extended Metaphor
As Sermon Vehicle

David Buttrick claims in his book *Homiletic,*

> *Preaching reaches for metaphorical language because
> God is a mysterious presence-in-absence. God is not an
> object in view. Therefore, preaching must resort to
> analogy, saying, "God is like. . . ." The language of
> analogy is profoundly related to fields of lived
> experience.*[1]

We read in Thomas Long's book *The Witness of Preaching,*

> *In a simple metaphor, we call something familiar by an
> unfamiliar name. We liken much talking to "a blizzard
> of words." In a simile, one thing is compared to another
> thing. In a metaphor, something is unexpectedly
> summoned to stand for something else. A metaphor seeks
> to create new meaning, to help us experience the reality
> of something in a new way. A simile is the tool of good
> teachers; a metaphor is the instrument of poets. There is
> mystery at the heart of the metaphor. It continues to tease
> our minds into active thought, urging us to discover more
> and more ways to revision what we thought we already
> saw well. Many of the parables of Jesus are metaphors
> in story form.*[2]

While we all understand the use of a single simple metaphor
to illustrate the truth we are trying to communicate in our sermon,
we often do not realize the tremendous edge a metaphor has for
communication when it is extended throughout the entire sermon.

An extended narrative metaphor begins with the real world. (See chapter 19 for an example sermon: "Judah's Song of Victory.") This is one of the most important reasons for using this speech technique to communicate the Gospel: We begin where people live. We begin where their minds are as they are seated after the hymn and watch us move into the pulpit for the proclamation. Instead of starting with camels, deserts, or fishermen around Galilee, we begin with the present real world. "We were all shocked last Tuesday as CBS announced that mother Linda Smith had murdered her own sons..." or "A huge ferry, *Estonia,* homeward bound to Stockholm, sunk off the coast of Finland in the Baltic Sea last week. 140 survivors, 820 drowned. Where was God?" or "I only had one pastor in my 60 years of life, Rev. Christian C. Wessel. He baptized me in that little Greenville, Ohio, congregation...."

It's necessary to build a case here for narrative form in preaching. Narrative is so much of what the Gospel is about, it is the most effective instrument to gain and continue interest all the way through the sermon. Listen to Richard Jensen: "Story preaching is related to the helping power of the Gospel in still another way. It doesn't teach me about help (didactic). It doesn't offer me help directly through a word hurled into my existence (proclamatory). Rather, I hear a story in which help happens. As a listening participant in the life of the story I recognize that this same sort of help is offered to me."[3] Notice how many of our national television networks have spawned television programs which are simply narratives strung together. *Sixty Minutes, 20/20, Eye-to-Eye, American Journal, Prime Time Live, Unsolved Mysteries, 48 Hours*, all use the narrative because they know it communicates and it's what people are interested in and will continue to watch.

The extended narrative metaphor that I'm advocating is actually redescribing reality. We certainly can find these metaphors in many of the biblical stories, in the newspapers of our day, the television shows mentioned above. Most helpful is the practice of keeping a homiletical journal in which we can write down those things that we see which are intriguing and of great interest. "To begin with, your best illustrations will come from your daily observation of men (*sic*) and things. Some ministers, I notice, possess books of illustrations neatly indexed under headings. If you have a 'noting eye,' you will find a much better and more living book in the first village and congregation where you are settled." [4]

While the extended metaphor is in the language of analogy, it is more than a simile which says something is like something. In a strong metaphor we move beyond just saying what it's like and into an area that is more poetic, creative, and experimental.

The extended narrative metaphor is much more than an illustration which makes more clear a truth. It is the vehicle that transports the listener and the preacher through the entire sermon. Only one is used in this kind of sermon so that there is no mixing of metaphors or distraction for the original one.

The correctly constructed extended metaphor sermon will keep a tension of that which is similar and that which is different in the comparison throughout the entire message. This tension can be handled in a playful way and sometimes even with good humor that will make the sermon contents sparkle. Henry Mitchell writes:

> *Just as it is true that figures or metaphors may be used in either the textual or the expositional sermon, and just as it is true that a whole sermon may be built in a single story, it is also true that a whole sermon may use a single metaphor. . . . The moves would simply be based in several parallels between the figure and human experience. I recall sermons on fishing — studying the fish habits, choosing the bait to match the taste of the fish sought, waiting with patience, and pulling in the fish — which acknowledged that to be caught for Christ is life, not death. The text, of course, would be "I will make you fishers of men" (Matthew 4:19).*[5]

Please allow the metaphor to carry itself throughout the sermon and refrain from any or very little explanation of it. Notice that when Jesus told his parables which were smaller metaphors, he hesitated to explain them at all. It was only on one occasion when he was really pressed that he did so and that may have not have been with the best results!

Hear the words of Charles E. Miller:

Jesus loved analogies and metaphors. That is why he asked himself while preparing to preach, "What is the kingdom of heaven like? To what shall I compare it?" Analogy is based on the principle that we proceed from the known to the unknown. It points out the similarities between what is already understood, appreciated, persuasive, or evident and what is not. An analogy makes an explicit comparison: "the kingdom of heaven is like a dragnet thrown into the sea." A metaphor makes only an implicit comparison, as when Jesus said, "I am the light of the world."[6]

Story is at the heart of the extended narrative metaphor. It seeks more and more ways to revision what we thought we saw well in the first place. This keeps the thought alive and brings it home over and over throughout the text. The mystery is obvious and thus keeps the listener attentive to hear it solved.

The extended metaphor is more poetic than other ways of speaking in the pulpit. It talks about a different way and a different world than is our present situation. The language of the metaphor is carried throughout the entire sermon. For instance, if the metaphor is about hunting geese on the Missouri River, hunting terms would be used throughout the entire sermon. Or if the story is from *Time* magazine about someone in Ohio seeing a vision of Christ on a corn crib wall, the language of corn crib and farm would be used throughout the text. Mitchell continues: "The advantage of figures or metaphors is not only the clarity of ideas as visualized, but also the possibility that the hearer will feel very close to the sport of fishing, for instance, and therefore become deeply involved in the message."[7]

What we're talking about is quite different from a sermon illustration and even a sermon illustration which is referred to several times throughout the sermon. It is an experience for the preacher and the listener. The sermon becomes an event and something that is experienced as well as understood. The preacher will often begin with a portion of a story and then will keep returning to that story and extending it further until it is told all the way through the sermon and concludes the sermon with a nice frame as it began.

One might say that this type of preaching gives a glimpse of God's kingdom and that we experience how it shall be and how it should be in the kingdom Jesus proclaimed. Arndt Halvorson puts it: "A sermon is a call to the depths of the human heart from the depths of the human heart."[8]

The story and metaphor is told in such a way that the hearer is invited in. One almost might say that it is seductive and that you simply cannot resist listening to it and wondering how it will come out as it carries you through the sermon event. The extended metaphor varies from an extended narrative in that the metaphor carries also the "is like" all the way through the message.

Someone has said that Christ is the "God with us" metaphor and I suspect that that would stand up if tested. I simply believe that because God is not visible in our presence we need metaphor and narrative to experience (not just learn about it!) God's presence with us now.

There are some risks in this type of preaching. The success of the sermon will rise or fall on the art of the preacher to tell story. The metaphor can also be so strong and call attention to itself that it nearly crushes the gospel truth and obscures the message that you're trying to communicate.

This kind of sermon simply cannot be read. A manuscript should not be taken into the pulpit when we're trying to do this kind of captivating storytelling and weaving of metaphor throughout it all. Ralph L. Lewis rolls out the big guns in *Persuasive Preaching*[9] to make the point.

> *American church goers long ago proved their preference for extemporaneous speaking. They want their preachers to prepare, but they do not want sermons read to them. The verdict is in favor of the spoken and against the read sermon; and it is no use arguing about it.*
>
> *Many objective studies have tested listener reactions to reading from a manuscript versus speaking extemporaneously with no more than notes for reference. Early*

tests revealed that listeners retain 36% more of the content when the message is delivered in extemporaneous speech. Tests repeatedly have found audience reactions more sympathetic and more attentive when speakers use direct extemporaneous speaking rather than manuscript reading.

"In most churches," says Buttrick, "a manuscript even dramatically read would be a barrier between preacher and people."[10]

The pew is unanimous in favor of extempore delivery, and the pew is right.[11]

The American people overwhelmingly favor the extemporaneous method. Most speakers forfeit effectiveness who choose any other.[12]

I would betray my strong feelings for not taking a manuscript into the pulpit unless I continued the argument a bit further using the words "Henry Ward Beecher, pastor of Plymouth Church in Brooklyn, with standing room only for forty years, said: 'a written sermon is apt to reach out like a gloved hand; an unwritten sermon reaches out the warm and glowing palm, bare to the touch.' "[13]

We must be careful lest the scripture is being forced to fit the analogy or that it actually distracts from the scripture. In other words, we have it all backwards if we find a clever metaphor we want to use and then try to force scripture to fit it.

Another risk we take in this kind of preaching is that it would lead to such free association that our listeners would be so involved that they would miss the focus of the sermon. Invariably when we tell story and metaphor from the pulpit the listeners engage in likening what they hear to their own life experience. That can be good most of the time but it can also lead to a sort of daydreaming that can't be penetrated by the preacher's finest art.

There are many more pluses in using the extended metaphor than there are negatives. Certainly the major reason for it is that it keeps interest and it invites our hearers into the experience of the Gospel. It begins where people are and it moves the message along subtly, coaxing and convincing the hearers. It provides a way to organize and remember the sermon content. It is a very persuasive way to preach.

I like it because I believe that much of the pulpit work in my own denomination has too much "head" and not enough "heart." I think that this kind of preaching appeals to the heart as well as the head.

It also aids in the listener internalizing the truth that we're trying to proclaim. When it's experienced as well as articulated with a memorable vehicle transporting it, the listener is more apt to believe it and remember it and apply it in daily life.

Sallie McFague claims that parables are extended metaphors. "That is what a reasonably good story will do: It will engage the reader or hearer in a metaphoric process in which reality is redescribed, a new world is disclosed, a challenge to transformation is extended by way of an invitation to enter this world, to see reality this way, and to adopt an appropriate way of being."[14]

Here is an actual copy of an extended narrative metaphor sermon outline which I took into the pulpit:

Introduction: Sabbatical in Liberia, West Africa
        Meeting Old Man Mopolu and Mama Gana
        "Wear the skin" metaphor
What's our belief about Jesus and God?
        Incarnation — Bethlehem to Jerusalem —
            Spirit
We are called to wear skin of Christ
Text Colossians 1:25 — Read from Bible
        Wear it as *servants*
        A congregation that does it
        All God's people have a ministry
        Saint Paul — Priesthood Luther —
            Reformation — Old Man
        Pastor more than Holy Person
        Church = meeting place for ministers — Mama
            Gana
Paul adds: proclaim Good News

Heartbeat of discipleship — witness
Side benefit of witnessing
So What? Put on, serve, witness, celebrate skin
Frame: Old Man and Mama Gana

1. David Buttrick, *Homiletic* (Philadelphia: Fortress Press, 1987), p. 116.

2. Thomas Long, *The Witness of Preaching* (Louisville: Westminster/John Knox Press, 1989), pp. 172-173.

3. Richard A. Jensen, *Telling the Story* (Minneapolis: Augsburg Publishing, 1980), p. 185.

4. James Black, *The Mystery of Preaching* (London: Marshall, Morgan, and Scott, 1977), p. 45.

5. Henry H. Mitchell, *Black Preaching: The Recovery of a Powerful Art* (Nashville: Abingdon Press, 1990), p. 89.

6. Charles E. Miller, C.M., *Ordained to Preach* (New York: Alba House, 1992), p. 41.

7. Mitchell, p. 119.

8. Arndt L. Halvorson, *Authentic Preaching* (Minneapolis: Augsburg Publication House, 1982), p. 9.

9. The following four citations are from: Ralph L. Lewis, *Persuasive Preaching Today* (Litho Crafters, Inc., 1979), p. 235.

10. Buttrick, *op. cit.*, pp. 162-163.

11. Watson, *op. cit.*, p. 271.

12. Abernathy, *op. cit.*, p. 271.

13. Arthur S. Phelps, *Speaking for Ministers* (Grand Rapids: Baker, 1964; Revised by DeKoster), p. 128.

14. Edward R. Riegert, *Imaginative Shock Preaching and Metaphor* (Burlington, Ontario: Trinity Press, 1990), p. 102.

Chapter 8

✧✧✧✧✧✧✧

Preaching For
Baby Boomers And Busters

The baby boomers, that group who were born just after World War Two, have been researched and studied and showcased in many, many ways. The result of that research indicates that boomers have not been going to church and that their children called busters may be coming back. This gives us motivation to prepare sermons which will not only proclaim the gospel effectively but also do it in a way which will be of interest and fit the needs of the boomer and buster generations. Using the following categories which are broad generalizations of the needs of busters and boomers, we can come up with our edge for the sermons which will be most effective for them.

Open to experience: Because the boomer very much wants to "feel" as well as "intellectually understand," we need to prepare the sermon event so that the heart will feel emotions and gospel truths as well as the mind accepting and understanding them. The preachers' sharing themselves, using verbal sanctions, emotionally loaded words, and stereotypes which express the heart as well as the intellect will be important. Extended narrative which invites the listener into the experience to feel it as well as understand it is crucial.

Help for practical living: Our sermon content must deal with the everyday struggle to survive in a very frantic and fragmented lifestyle. How we get and distribute our money, parent our children, relate to our parents, enrich our job as vocation is the sort of thing this generation wants to hear.

Opportunity for healthy relationships: The stories, illustrations, and metaphors that we use need to include relating to other people.

In a day of individualization and privatization our sermon must help the listener establish healthy relationships and must present the possibility of being part of God's family as that kind of relationship.

Doing as well as believing: This means that the "so what" of our message will need to be carefully thought out so that practical first steps will be given because of the truths we have proclaimed from the pulpit.

Informal and shared ministry: The vocabulary in our preaching must be simple language and must indicate a collegial partnership in the ministry of Christ and the church. It needs to be presented as *our* ministry rather than the preacher's ministry. A certain informality in the pulpit will be attractive also. Easy to understand language and the removal of preacher "shop talk" will help convey this attitude.

Understanding the modern family: In composing our message we must not assume that our hearers are living in family units as they did in days gone by. Many will be single parents trying to raise their family by themselves, many will be divorced parents remarrying and now raising blended families. They will probably rarely gather as a family around the meal table. Television will be their primary source of communication with the world. So the sermon will need to give practical advice, support the family unit, and help couples with their struggle to stay married in a very complicated time.

Champion of diversity: The language we use must be inclusive language sensitive to the many races and nationalities to whom we will be preaching. It's important to carefully eliminate any comments or words that would even hint towards a racist attitude or contribute to ageism and classism and intellectualism. Women want to be treated as equals and many of us men are determined that that shall be so. The sermon illustrations and examples must indicate it.

Meaningful worship: The baby boomer generation's top priority with religion is to "be put in touch with the supernatural." This certainly means that our preaching must be a spiritual experience as well as correct information being conveyed and witness taking place. Through narratives, our eloquence and witness to the presence of Jesus Christ in the world, the sermon ought to indicate that something significant between God and God's people is taking place while the preacher is preaching.

Lots of action: Of course the sermon must be short, have movement, call for change from the status quo, with lots of appropriate gestures and a high energy level of the preacher. Long, involved sentences and repetition of thought won't be tolerated by the boomers and busters. Work for movement in the vocabulary you use, the organization of the sermon, and your own body language.

The above categories of boomers are very much included in what their children, the baby busters, are demanding as well. Also, they seem to indicate that they want the message to be interesting and lively. It cannot be a lecture on theology. Well thought out humor will be very much appreciated. Long, involved, dry truths, no matter how compelling the logic, will not reach the baby buster generation.

They also want the sermon to be very relevant and to deal with right now issues. Our extended metaphor sermons must get the latest metaphor possible from the latest newspaper, television nightly news, situation comedies, or news magazines.

Not unlike the baby boomers, their children want sermons which are important to life now. Close to the ground connections offering some "how to's" and asking for input from the congregation and those outside the church will work for the busters. It will help to find out from the present membership of the congregation and especially from those outside the church what are the important things in their life right now and then relate the gospel to them.

There is yet another tricky issue that busters want from returning to church. They want to feel like they're joining others of their age. We older preachers will have to be careful that the examples and narratives and metaphors that we select for our preaching reflect a lifestyle presently in the buster generation. Referring to significant others, uplinks and downlinks and meeting on-line will be verbiage they understand and appreciate. The principal characters in stories we tell from the pulpit must include the twenty and thirty-year-olds as well.

William L. Malcomson writes timely advice to us as we take a measure of those to whom we preach:

1. Some people are crying out for direction and guidance — they want guidance from the One who put this world together.

2. Many want inspiration, a lift, an injection of power or strength, perhaps they need courage.

3. There are a large number of people who want peace, security, serenity and comfort. They want to be filled with the radiance of tranquility.

4. They want to be wanted. That they can contribute something; that other people are interested in what they have to offer.

5. They want a religion that is undemanding. Since what they want is a neat, complete, well-rounded existence, a little bit of religion helps round them out.

6. There are those who want a demanding religion — a religion that requires their complete devotion. They want a cross to carry.

7. Many people are easily bored. The service is out there and up there; what they want is action. They want to be involved.

8. We all know people who are religious dilettantes. Give them something different and they are happy.

9. A number of people are afraid, panicked, scared to death by life. They need hope — certain hope right now.

10. Some believe in nothing. They cannot believe anything is worth doing. They want evidence to the contrary, but they probably wouldn't accept it as valid.

11. Have you noticed that most people seem to know a lot less about the Bible and theology than does the preacher? Theology is assumed to be something for specialists. They might like to hear more about the Bible and theology, but they would not necessarily accept what the preacher says.

12. There are people who want to be talked down to. They rejoice in saying, "woe is me." Somehow this seems to them to help them deal with their guilt.

13. Other people bristle at the slightest hint of condescension. They want to be talked up to.

14. Preachers are often alarmed to discover that the people in the congregation know a lot more about life than does the preacher. They do know much more about their own lives and the world. What they do not know is the relation of the Bible to real life, the Gospel to life. If a preacher tries to please all types of people, he will say absolutely nothing that helps anyone and will certainly be dishonest with himself.[1]

---

1. William L. Malcomson, *The Preaching Event* (Philadelphia: Westminster Press, 1968), pp. 48, 49, & 50.

Chapter 9

✧✧✧✧✧✧✧

Local History As Gospel Parable

In my 35 years of preaching I never found a sermon series in which the congregation and community had more interest than those I did on local history. I used it as a source of contemporary parables.

The folklore, history, and tales that have been related from one generation to another in a community and often times written down for posterity, make excellent vehicles for transporting the gospel message in your preaching. To announce that you will give a series of sermons based on the stories and histories of the area where you are preaching is almost guaranteed to attract people to listen.

To add to the interest, a committee of the congregation can prepare the bulletin covers which would go along with each of the sermon themes. Old pictures from the local historical society or county library will work well. A person affected by the story, a descendant of the heroine or hero of the story, or someone who would have some kind of connection to the story no matter how remote, will add flavor and interest if they are in attendance at the worship service when the sermon is preached.

These stories serve as parables to lay along the gospel truth that you want to proclaim. In the best sense of the word they serve as structure for extended narrative metaphor sermons. They will meet the criteria of Walter Burghardt when he writes: "What I am commending to the preacher is a spirituality that is biblically based — and especially so. Not simply the study of Old Testament and New Testament spirituality, though this can base the broader life of the spirit. Rather, a reverent immersion in Scripture such that intelligence is subservient to love."[1]

To offer this kind of sermon series will demonstrate to your congregation that you own their heritage and this community into which God has called you to be a preacher. It will show respect and interest in the locality. The people will love you for that. It also will invite others in the community to attend your worship service and hear again, or for the first time, about their community's heritage.

Sermon series on local history are often best received soon after you begin as preacher in a new congregation. It helps the preacher be incorporated into that local culture and establishes a reputation for preaching which is interesting and worthwhile.

Local stories, folklore, and tales told from one generation to the next in a community can often be found in the local public library. Often you will find a more informal file of local history and the more noteworthy events that took place in the community's background. Of course there is almost always the county history that has been written and published and is available and full of this kind of stories.

The local genealogical society will also be a rich source for local history and stories. The county historical society, another resource often organized and cared for by older volunteers who love to relate what they know about the background of the community, will be very helpful.

In many counties there are older people who frequent the county courthouse and its public areas. Sit with them and ask about the famous stories of the community. They will be all too happy to share them with you.

There are almost always one or two people in the community who have the respect and the title of local historian. Make an appointment to visit and take your tape recorder. Ask them to relate those stories. They will often provide you with a booklet or booklets that have been published from time to time which relate the history of the community, tell about its founding, and relate stories about its famous persons. Many organizations publish historical booklets on observances of anniversaries which include some wonderful pictures that can be used as bulletin covers when you relate the history story.

Some of the themes for a sermon series like this might be local composers of religious music, or the "first" in the area like: first settler, first child born in the county, first clergy to arrive, first school teacher, first doctor. The "firsts" can go on and on.

Other possible themes for a series could be around the stories of the nineteenth century, stories of the county, state parables, state psalms relating the music composed and published from natives,[2] and a tour of the county or city.

A couple examples of how to organize this kind of local parable sermon are:

1. Begin the local story.
2. Relate the gospel truth — scripture.
3. Continue the story as example.
4. Give an up-to-date application of the gospel.
5. Finish the local story.
6. Some action steps of gospel truth to be taken.
7. The conclusion and a teaser for next sermon.

or

1. Tell most of the story.
2. Draw an analogy to the gospel.
3 Call for specific action to be taken.
4. Tell the end of the story.

Here are some examples of local history that I found work well in presenting this kind of sermon series:

•Jessie Hyatt of Winterset, Iowa, who developed the Delicious Apple from which all others come; we talked about Jesus as the vine and us as the branches and about the roots of Christianity.

•The night a young girl saved a train; we talked about making a sacrifice for others and the supreme sacrifice Jesus made for us.

•A giant that was carved out of gypsum to fool the people; we talked about what genuine discipleship was all about.

•The time a church bell was stolen and buried; we talked about the joy in being Christian and what can steal it from us.

•The rumor of buried gold; we talked about locating our treasure.

•The night some men blew up the courthouse; we talked about the dynamite of the Gospel.

•The hobo convention held in Britt, Iowa; our undeserved Eucharistic banquet.

•The time they couldn't stop the flow of an artesian well; about how God's grace flows freely through the waters of our baptism.[3] (See in this book, sample sermon: "Belle Plaine's Gusher.")

Of course, this kind of preaching can be overdone and ought to be used sparingly. However, especially upon arrival in a new parish when you need to understand the people and culture into which you have been called and you need to gain credibility with those who hear your preaching, it is an excellent device to hold the gospel before your people and to integrate yourself into their community.

Richard Jensen, in his book *Telling the Story*, gives the following additional suggestions for creating stories for preaching:

1. Always begin with a text — our interest is not in the creative potential of our own story telling ability. We are concerned with recasting a biblical text so that it might come alive for our hearers in new ways.

2. Grace can only be portrayed in the lives of real people. Use stories that involve people that our hearers can identify with. The incarnation stands as the clue to our storytelling.

3. Your autobiography can be an effective method of story preaching. Our hearers may be enabled to see themselves by induction.

4. Know the difference between allegory and parable when you create a story. An allegory is a story that has several points of correspondence of things already known. Parables strive toward a simple conclusion. They seek to capture the central experience of the text.

5. Visual clues may enhance greater listener participation in your story. Art, hymns, items in bulletin, shepherd's staff, a person from the area in which the story takes place may all help.

6. Create situations for the "overhearing" of the gospel. Children's sermons can be a good example. At a funeral, words are overheard which are told primarily to the family.

7. A simple way to begin story preaching is by creating stories that parallel the biblical text and let the congregation make the connections between text and story.

8. The use of silence can be an effective way to involve people in your sermon.

9. Biblical texts should be meditated on in the light of stories we know from literature, theater, movies, television, and so forth. This is called vertical exegesis. It thinks about a given text in relation to other stories that you know. This aspect of vertical exegesis does its homework in pastoral calling and visitation. These are living stories all around you.

Surely the best preaching we do is that preaching where text (horizontal exegesis) and people (vertical exegesis) meet in creative encounter.[4]

1. Walter J. Burghardt, S.J., *Preaching: The Art and the Craft* (New York: Paulist Press, 1987), p. 87.

2. A series like this was published by the author titled *Iowa Psalms* (Lima, OH: CSS Publishing Co. Inc.).

3. This series of local history sermons has been published by the author titled *Iowa Parables* (Lima, OH: CSS Publishing Co., Inc.).

4. Richard Jensen, *Telling the Story* (Minneapolis: Augsburg/Fortress Press, 1980), pp. 151-158.

Chapter 10

❖❖❖❖❖❖❖

Preaching On Controversial Subjects

Fred Craddock has written: "We will know power has returned to the pulpit when and where preaching effects transformation in the lives of men and in the structures of society. There are reasons to believe that this renewal is not far away."[1]

There's no way to escape the fact we preachers are called to deal with issues upon which the congregation cannot and will not agree. In addition to giving comfort and encouragement, we must also be prophetic as is modelled by the prophets in the Bible. In whatever community we live there will be social issues that need to be addressed. It's our task to expose ugly sin, when we can locate it, to the light of day in the pulpit.

I don't believe it's a good idea to deal with controversial issues as soon as you arrive at your parish. Give your people time to learn to trust you. Have ample dialogue on many things with them, one to one, before bringing up these issues from the pulpit. Some of the things we're going to have to deal with over the next years will be: abortion, homosexuality, ecology, divorce, capital punishment, criminal justice, conscientious objection, immigration issues, and health care.

Do be very careful about politicians. They're trying to get elected or re-elected and will often want you and the church to support them in a position. They often approach the church in a very pragmatic and utilitarian way.

Sometimes sermons on controversial issues and social justice are better received by a congregation if there is a series of them. By all means don't surprise the congregation with the subject. Announce you're going to do it ahead of time and ask for their prayers as you prepare. It's very important to represent both sides of an issue fairly. This means that we construct our sermon in a way that we don't corner those who disagree with us in a situation where they're not able to have dialogue and speak back. The audience reaction based outline will work well for most of this kind of preaching. (See page 45 for a diagram.)

It's one of the truisms of the Christian faith that Christians, steeped in scripture, can come to different conclusions about the same social issue and ethical practice. Allow for it. It will help immensely when planning to give a sermon on a controversial issue if you will provide ways that congregants can ask questions, dialogue and discuss with you and each other as response to the sermon. This might be a forum or discussion group after the worship service.

Your voice ought to be very conversational and not at all haranguing or mean-spirited or scolding.

It is important to try to find a way through a very hot issue so that no one loses face, but people have the freedom and are motivated to change their attitude and behavior. You just haven't gained anything if you drive out those who don't agree with you. The goal is to change attitudes and behavior of your hearers while faithfully proclaiming and applying the Gospel. It's our edge.

One of the best ways to give integrity to the subjects you address from the pulpit is to ask for suggestions from the congregation as to what they would like to hear preached and addressed.

It's important to avoid the "straw man" technique. In argumentation there is a technique of erecting a straw man and then destroying it in front of the people in order to gain prestige with them. This doesn't work in preaching. There's no need to be a martyr in the pulpit if it's not necessary.

Flood the worship service with prayers for guidance and take that very seriously. Admit right up front that dealing with this subject makes you very nervous and that you're doing it out of a deep feeling of conscience, hopeful that your listeners will continue to love you regardless of how you come out on the issue. Seek the guidance of scripture and quote it liberally. Make your own witness in a humble way, being careful not to indicate that anybody who disagrees with you is surely un-Christian and "on their way to hell."

If it is true, admit it makes you nervous and very uncomfortable to deal with this particular subject but feel you must do so.

You can address the traps of a single issue mind and plead with people not to do that. Avoid labeling any side as "liberal, conservative, radical, bigots" and so forth — all inflammatory words. Emotionally loaded words will only drive the people away rather than coax them into changing their mind.

For God's sake and for your sake and for the congregation's sake, find some good humor for relief of tension and use it frequently throughout the sermon! It's our edge.

In the worship bulletin provide additional materials on the subject that you encourage your people to study.

Quote others in your denomination or any study or statement the church has made on the subject as a further resource for God's people.

The great preacher Phillips Brooks said in his *Eight Lectures on Preaching:* "Never sacrifice your reverence for truth to your desire for usefulness. Say nothing which you do not believe to be true because you think it may be helpful. Keep back nothing which you do not believe to be true because you think it may be harmful."[2]

Some controversial issues are better discussed in forums and seminars rather than proclaimed from the pulpit. However, there will be those justice issues when you'll need to take the heat that comes from addressing people who are comfortable and would rather not be confronted with the Christian ethic of their behavior. In those cases, preach confident that you follow in a train of saints who have done so before you. Be firm and loving and remember the preacher's edge will work for you in the preaching and in the hearing of the sermon. Count on it.

---

1. Fred B. Craddock, *As One Without Authority* (Nashville: Abingdon Press, 1983), p. 21.

2. Phillips Brooks, *Eight Lectures on Preaching* (Speck, 1959), p. 271.

Chapter 11

❖❖❖❖❖❖❖

The Sermon On The Amount: Stewardship From The Pulpit[1]

One of the more frightening tasks we preachers have, particularly as we're getting started in our parish ministry, is preaching regularly on the subject of financial stewardship. For some reason a myth prevails that there is something sacred about our money and we shouldn't mention it from the pulpit. As a matter of fact, if we put a fence around the pulpit and do not address financial stewardship, we are eliminating about two-thirds of our congregants' lives, lifestyles, worries, and that subject about which they are most interested in hearing. It's relevant to them right where they live. It's our edge.

Here are some ideas I have about preaching that "sermon on the amount." You will notice similarities with preaching on controversial subjects. It ought to be done well and with confidence as a witness from us and the Almighty to our people.

We ought to talk about our own struggles and need for growth. That way we are not preaching down to our congregational members, but rather are inviting them to join us in thinking through this subject and trying to grow with us.

Let the message be Bible-centered. I always made sure that I read the scripture in the pulpit from a Bible I could hold in my hand so that visually people knew where the message was coming from and my source of authority for saying what I was saying. Be very careful about proof-texting. Especially in stewardship preaching, it is easy to prove what you already wanted to say by looking up Bible verses that support it. Rather, take one of the great parables, miracles, or sayings of Jesus or Paul, or other early saints of the church, and let your message flow from that. It's an edge we have as preachers.

I doubt that we get very far by emphasizing duty when it comes to stewardship! I think it is much more effective to talk about the joy and privilege that is ours who have so much and for whom God has done so much and given so much, to be able to give to others.

Be sure to use specific terms which everybody understands, such as cash, dollars, credit cards, checkbooks, IRA's, savings accounts, and so forth. I think that "time, talent, and treasure" is an old chestnut that's out of date!

Be very careful not to scold, lecture, or belittle. Speak very kindly and non-judgmentally. Try to accept all where they are and then plead in a very persuasive way for some growth.

Be sure to use sizeable doses of humor and refrain from heaping on more guilt. It's so easy to harangue and build guilt on our people because they are not doing what they should or not doing what you are doing. Humor is good relief from that, and it is also a very persuasive and consistent method of teaching about the gospel with its privileges and responsibilities.

This means using the law very sparingly and talking a great deal about the gospel with great delight. Let enthusiasm show through. We ought to allow the spirit to set us free to preach with conviction and excitement about this wonderful subject that can give such significance and integrity to our lives.

By all means, if we are like most preachers and rather uncomfortable talking about the subject of stewardship in the pulpit, we ought to tell our people that. They'll love to hear us admit that we are human and that this is rather frightening for us to do, and they'll root for us to do it well!

Encourage reasonable increases in growth and Christian giving. Don't use examples that people will feel are unreachable. Acknowledge where *you* are and what *you* are trying to aim for, and plead for them to get started in growing, too.

Much of the above would not be frightening, and certainly our preaching would have more integrity and relation to the gospel, if we dealt with the subject of stewardship year-round. This means to talk about the subjects of stewardship of all God's creation as caretakers of the earth and its resources, of our own bodies and health, of our abilities and skills, and of our call through our baptism to be ministers all week long. The possible subjects can go on and on, and it can enrich our preaching, making it much more relevant than ignoring the subject except for one Sunday during the year.

Be very careful about making appeals of loyalty to church, preacher, or budget. This kind of stewardship pledging and giving is often very fickle and short-term. It is much more important that we talk about each person's *need to give* rather than any institution's *need to have* what we give. In a culture like ours we do have a big need to give lots of our income away in order to experience the integrity of being a Christian and to feel good about our priorities. Just be sure that God's love shines through and that the wonderful amazing grace that we talk about in every other facet of our lives is also applied in our stewardship and stewarding.

Be cautious about promising results such as prosperity or making an appeal to give because "we never had it so good." It could be that some seated there and others who will hear your message are not having it that good right now!

One of the main responsibilities in financial stewardship preaching is to lift the vision and stretch the possibilities, helping the congregation imagine what might be as we all work together to grow in this concept. Remember that people give in proportion to their grasp of the need; the quality of information provided; the amount of spiritual depth and motivation they have; the financial resources they have to share; and/or perhaps from your own example.

We so often forget in our preaching of any kind to suggest to our people the possible first steps as a result of that which we have learned in this instructive sermon. I call it the "so what!" of a sermon. Think through carefully what it would mean for each of us, because of these truths that you proclaim this day, and let your people hear it.

Several times a year in our preaching we have to remove the mystery regarding the writing of wills and doing estate planning and setting up trusts and endowments. We need to convince our people that this is, indeed, an easy thing to accomplish and a good practice of stewardship of our resources in order that future generations might continue to benefit because of our depth of faith and our willingness to share.

There are few things that can so enrich preaching and make it relevant and exciting to do as practicing the art of stewardship preaching year-round. In a culture such as ours where money talks and is the language of all the media and our lives, where our edge is to be close to the ground in our preaching and also faithful to the scripture we proclaim, we must continue to preach the sermon on the amount.

---

1. Jerry Schmalenberger, *Plane Thoughts on Parish Ministry* (Lima, Ohio: CSS Publishing Co., Inc., 1994).

Chapter 12

✧✧✧✧✧✧✧

Enriching And Polishing The Message

Sometimes the hardest part of sermon preparation and experiencing the edge which is ours is simply getting started. Here are some ideas that might prompt you to begin the task:

•Read over the scripture propers appointed for the day if you are pastor in a church that follows the church year. See the connections between the Old Testament lesson appointed for the day and the Gospel.

•Look at the New Testament lesson and see if there is a special emphasis that is needed from the pulpit of your congregation this week. Often the New Testament lesson does not connect with the Old Testament or the Gospel for the day.

•Think about the season of the church year you are in and what its general theme is and how that fits with the scripture appointed for the day.

Before you begin you'll want to consider the options of kinds of sermons from which you might select one and prepare:

•A textual three points and a poem.
•A people's sermon.
•A dialogue sermon.
•A sermon drama.
•A letter sermon.
•An extended metaphor sermon.
•An audience reaction sermon.
•A sermon based on a hymn.
•A simple narrative sermon.

Thomas G. Long in his excellent book on preaching, *The Witness of Preaching,* lists the following sermon forms that are frequently used. If you go through them while you're getting started, they can prime the pump and give you some ideas for an appropriate focus and way of organizing.

1. If this . . . then this . . . and thus this.
2. This is true . . . in this way . . . and also in this way . . . and in this other way, too.
3. This is the problem . . . this is the response of the gospel . . . these are the implications.
4. This is the promise of the Gospel — here is how we may live out that promise.
5. This is the historical situation in the text . . . these are the meanings for us now.
6. Not this . . . or this . . . or this . . . or this . . . but this.
7. Here is a prevailing view . . . but here is the claim of the Gospel.
8. This . . . but what about this? Well, then this. Yes, but what about this? And so on.
9. Here is a story: simple story; story reflection. Part of a story; reflection; rest of the story; issue; story.
10. This? Or that?[1]

Some other places to look for resources in enriching and polishing the sermon would be *Newsweek* and *Time* magazine cover stories. The inside few pages of these weekly news magazines often have very brief stories which cover in capsule form the entire content of that issue.

> *As you start your story hunt look for anecdotes that fire your thinking and stimulate your imagination. Vignettes that reveal human nature or the way the world works as you perceive it. Jot them down in your story journal. As you collect stories, you will automatically develop good listening skills, and you will discover the principles of good story telling. As you add to your repertoire, make adjustments and amendments that suit your style.*[2]

Your local newspaper is probably your best source of finding stories that can be used to serve as a vehicle and metaphor for the Gospel message.

Perhaps it would help to get started by trying to put the message in four or five phrases much like those which used to appear on Burma Shave signs. An old example would be: "How odd of God to choose the Jews."

Consider a hymn verse on which you could base or organize the gospel message. The congregation or you could sing it several times throughout the sermon.

Another way to get started would be to talk directly or on the phone to some of the people in your community and congregation to ask their opinion about this Gospel text and what ought to be said to the people of your community this Sunday.

Of course, commentaries can help open up the significance of the scripture. William Barclay's *Daily Study Bible* series is still probably one of the best helps in getting the context of the Bible passages.

Consider if there might be a visual aid or aids that can be displayed during your preaching. If the sermons of former pastors of the parish have been preserved in the archives, you might want to see what they said on this particular Sunday of the church year and quote them.

After your sermon has been written, go through it and see if you could enrich it by using a couple figures of speech like alliteration, which means the repetition of a particular sound. Other possible figures of speech are repeating the last words in the next sentence, defining something in terms of what it is not, using contrast of words, addressing an abstract quality, or using a number of sentences beginning with the same word or phrase. Use some words whose pronounced sound reflects their meaning. This is called *onomatopoeia*.

There's nothing wrong with repetition in a sermon. In fact, you'll probably want to be sure that the main thought is repeated several times and ways throughout the message. Repeating an individual word which can be remembered after the people leave the worship service is also a good technique. Similar to that would be repeating similar word endings.

Some preachers find asking a question and then answering it works well if it's not overdone. I especially like to use words that when pronounced suggest their meaning. So, a quaver in our voice indicates fear. When we describe the wind we use such terms as "whoosh."

Giving human form to inanimate objects can polish the sermon and be an effective way of communicating. Of course, the old standby of using similes is still worth trying. This simply means we tell the similarity between two objects using such words as "like" and "as if" and "so."

After the sermon has been prepared, you might want to ask the following questions that can serve as a screen through which you put your sermon in order that you use the preacher's edge and use as effective language and speech communication techniques as possible. Ask yourself:

•Have I been inclusive in my language?
•Is my vocabulary understandable to fifth graders?
•Have I left room for inspiration in the pulpit?
•Have I included implications for our congregation?
•Have I acknowledged vital concerns of people this week?
•Is there more of God's grace than God's law?
•Have I made my own witness?
•Is there some humor for relief throughout the sermon?
•Does the sermon acknowledge the season of the church year?
•Is "so what" answered with specific, clear steps to take?
•Does the sermon start where people are?
•Are there places where it would be more interesting if I used figures of speech?
•What one thing do I believe God wants them to remember?
•Have I been faithful to the scripture text?

1. Thomas Long, *The Witness of Preaching* (Louisville: Westminster/John Knox Press, 1989), pp. 127-9.

2. Roy Alexander, *Power Speech* (New York: Amacon, American Management Association, 1986), p. 157.

Chapter 13

❖❖❖❖❖❖❖

Sermons For Children[1]

For whom do we give the children's sermon? What is the message we are attempting to convey? Is there an edge for preacher and listener here also? And, most important, why do we do it at all?

After preaching 1,400 children's sermons, I am not sure that the message we give can be learned by the ones who come forward for it. I doubt they will even remember it for the remainder of that day, and I am certain the purpose must be more than the content of the message. Still, congregations demand that children's sermons be given and often comment that it is the most meaningful and understandable part of all the verbal messages in our worship!

After observing many students and pastors trying to satisfy their congregation's demand for children's sermons, I am convinced that some ought never give them. In fact, as a homiletician, I am not even sure that a student can learn to do children's sermons very well. Some seem to be born to the task. Truly, it is more like a gift than a set of acquired skills. The weariness I experience with a lot of the children's sermons I hear leads me to advise that some preachers should take advantage of someone in the congregation (like an experienced pre-school teacher) who can do it well, and then sit with the kids and listen.

Neither am I sure that those young people who come forward for the sermon have the capacity to relate the utilized object to the lesson or truth the object is supposed to illustrate. However, I do believe the object ought to be used as something to focus on and to playfully wonder and talk about.

After all these years of giving children's sermons, I am convinced that the time is probably best spent in helping children feel included, valued, important, and loved in and by the congregation. Hence, it is more important to provide a certain "feel of it" than to get content understood. It is a time for the pastor to bond with the children of the congregation. It is the children's time in the liturgy when the congregation acknowledges they are a part of God's family, and it is a time when God's love and that of the people around them — especially their pastor — is communicated to them.

The time might even better be named "Children's Time," when the children look forward to some fun and playfulness within the setting of the worship experience and when they have friendship demonstrated and expressed to them. It will be a time the children anticipate each week that is for and about them.

Of course, overhearing does take place. It is an opportunity for the adults to hear further illustrative material about what will be proclaimed in the other sermon of the day. Certainly the children's sermon ought to support that one and recognize the theme of the liturgy and worship.

The children's sermon is not a time to display how cute children are. With this in mind, we need to pay particular attention to which way the children face and which way the pastor faces. We must also note the pastor's posture to be sure he or she does not tower over the children, yet still conveys the office of pastor. Some pastors kneel to speak and others sit to be at the children's level. My advice is not to ask questions of the children or force an enthusiastic "good morning" if they do not want to do that.

Story is probably the best form for a children's sermon. The old fashioned flannel graph or the opportunity for children to act out the story in the Old Testament or Gospel for the day is still a very effective way of communicating and enjoying a certain playfulness and creativity during the children's time.

There are other ways we might consider helping children not just to endure, but actually enjoy, coming to church. Booster chairs such as those used in restaurants, stacked up at the door and available for the children as they go into the worship area, can enable them to see more than the back of a pew and observe the activity in front of the church, and thus enjoy the service more. The old fashioned "children of the church" when young people are dismissed during part of the service for their own special worship opportunity still works. Many parents enjoy worship without having to tend to children the entire time (or part of the time). Most growing congregations find that a Sunday school held at the same time as worship works very well.

Why we do it, to whom our message is addressed, and what that message is are all crucial questions to be considered and answered as we decide whether or not to call young people forward for a children's sermon.

---

1. Jerry Schmalenberger, *Plane Thoughts on Parish Ministry* (Lima, Ohio: CSS Publishing Co., Inc., 1994).

Transition

✧✧✧✧✧✧✧

As we move from consideration of the sermon to its delivery, we examine the results of research on listening which ought to influence how we present the message.

1. Researchers have found that people stop listening when the material is uninteresting. They pay attention only to the material they find stimulating.

2. Distorting a person's message often occurs when the speaker's delivery is poor. Listeners are influenced more by the delivery than by the truth of the message.

3. Closely related to message delivery is the fact that people tend to be influenced more by the dramatic emotional elements of a sermon than by its logical elements.

4. Becoming overstimulated or emotionally involved with the speaker also can create message distortion. If, for example, a parishioner should question a pastor's integrity as a person, it would not be easy to remain open to what is being said.

5. Most listeners find it difficult to separate the essential from the non-essential in a message.

6. Mentally jumping ahead of the person speaking can cause one to miss part of the message — perhaps an essential of its meaning.

7. A person can think at a rate of more than four hundred words per minute. But speakers rarely talk at a pace of more than two hundred. So the listener thinks ahead of the speaker and misses part of the message.

8. A common obstacle to effective listening is faked attention.

9. Often people allow emotion-laden words to block their listening. Poor listeners respond to the loaded words rather than to their contextual meanings.

10. Effective listening is blocked when personal prejudices and deep-seated convictions impair comprehension and understanding.[1]

When we take these findings about our listeners seriously, it ought to help us deliver a sermon which will be vital, interesting, inspirational and remembered. Let's look at some practical tips of what to do and not to do when we preach.

---

1. Myron R. Chartier, *Preaching as Communication* (Abingdon Preacher's Library, 1981), p. 53.

Chapter 14

❖❖❖❖❖❖❖

Warming Up The Message
And The Messenger

Homer K. Buerlein writes: "Many a sermon is given a magnificent aura by the infectious nature of the preacher and a skillful delivery. But what bothers me are those dutifully researched and composed sermons that are totally devoid of a pleasingly persuasive and appealing presentation."[1]

If you're really serious about doing the best possible delivery of your sermon, you will make the effort to practice it out loud before delivery. Here are some suggestions that may prove helpful in getting the most out of that warm-up session.

Go into the worship space where you will be delivering the sermon and spend a time of prayer before the altar presenting this message to God and asking for God's spirit's guidance. Pray yourself full and think of the work you've done on your sermon as a gift you're now offering up to God.

Be certain that you practice reading the gospel upon which the sermon is going to be based as well as practicing the sermon. Reading scripture can be very effective communication if simple principles of lecture recital and oral interpretation of literature are practiced. To be even more effective, memorize the gospel and communicate it to your congregation without reading it.

With no one in the room, try to duplicate the preaching situation as best you can. If you preach from a pulpit, use that pulpit and if you use a public address system, turn it on just as it will be when the congregation is in attendance.

Put yourself under the same time, articulation and audience reaction pressure as if the congregation were all seated there watching you warm up yourself and the sermon. This is important.

You'll not get nearly the benefit out of the warm-up if you cheat in that empty sanctuary. Go all the way through the message without stopping just as if it were the real thing.

In order to give your sermon energy and allow the feeling portion to be felt, overact with your voice projection and your energy and gestures. Eventually, when you give the sermon in front of your congregation, the natural stage fright will compensate enough to calm this down. But for now, let your arms flail and make many wild gestures.

> *It is possible to exercise the gesture impulse, and to cultivate the gesture habit. The theoretical foundation for such belief is the James-Lang theory of emotions, which has been fully and finally demonstrated. The theory is that a feeling can be accentuated by the physical expression of that particular feeling. In other words, we are afraid because we run, angry because we strike.* [2]

Paul Brees writes advice to preachers who have difficulty getting their hands and arms to gesture:

> *In walking through a graveyard at midnight, alone, just as you are in the middle of a collection of ghostly, white tombstones, start to run. Trot slowly at first, then increase your speed — and you will find yourself thoroughly frightened and probably running at top speed before you get out.*
>
> *If we took this theory to the pulpit, we will have the basis for the gesture habit. Force yourself in a warm-up session to exaggerate your gestures. Swing your arms and shake your fists. The impulse to gesture will respond to exercise. Next time you deliver the sermon it should be natural to make gestures at the appropriate place.* [3]

Use your voice to its fullest capacity, projecting it out across the room or into the microphone as if you had the most important thing in the world to convey to these people and wanted to be sure that they heard it and knew that you believed it strongly.

I like to imagine the congregation is in their place and that I know where certain members will be seated. I look at them and imagine their reaction and move my eye contact from one part of the sanctuary to another, remembering whom I will be addressing.

If you must take a manuscript into the pulpit (and I do not recommend it), use that manuscript the first time through, go through the sermon again with a very scanty outline, and then try with God's help to do it without any notes at all!

Because we are an educated clergy and carry with us a certain distinction and sophistication, I do believe most of our preaching errs on the side of being bland and delivered with very little enthusiasm. So I recommend the above warming-up the sermon in order to realize the full possibility of our oratory technique and break out of the often dull lecture style that we develop.

Because it's rather frightening to stand in front of a congregation no matter how many times we've done it, we can always count on that holding us back somewhat in expressing our emotion and excitement about this good gospel. That's why I strongly recommend we take the step of "overacting" from the pulpit in this warm-up session.

I believe the same is true with the use of a manuscript when we're by ourselves and not under the pressure of many faces upturned to hear what we have to say. We think we can keep our eyes away from the manuscript enough to have good eye contact with the congregation and also allow enough spontaneity at the time we deliver the sermon. However, that old fear gnaws away at our bellies and for security we rapidly retreat to reading the manuscript. Not in every case, but in many, that will cause us to be less than enthusiastic and rarely have eye contact with those to whom we preach, and a rather monotone or holy tone delivery sets in (some call this the stained glass voice).

We will probably become our best at preaching when we have learned to develop a two-track mind as we deliver the sermon. The great preachers I know all describe the ability to have one portion of their mind be thinking about what words they will say to convey this gospel, and another track of their mind thinking and observing what adjustments need to be made because of the way the sermon is being received (or not being received) by the congregation. A warm-up session can help us develop these two tracks mentally as we deliver the sermon without the pressure of the congregation being there.

Back at Wittenberg College years ago my debate teacher, G. Vernon Kelley, would have us all deliver our speech at the same time in the same room in very loud voices. It was called roar practice. He would even walk around the room and question us right in our face, eye-to-eye, as we were trying to concentrate on giving our speech. His theory was that we had to develop these two tracks: one that focused on content and delivery, the other which focused on how the speech was being accepted and the necessary adjustments we needed to make while we were speaking. I have taken that technique into my homiletics courses. It has shocked the students and other faculty in the vicinity, but I do believe it begins to develop the two-track preacher and gives us an edge in communicating the Gospel effectively.

---

1. Homer K. Buerlein, *How to Preach More Powerful Sermons* (Philadelphia: Westminster Press, 1986), p. 1.

2. Paul R. Brees and G. Vernon Kelley, *Modern Speaking* (Fairborn, OH: The Miami Valley Publishing Co., 1953), pp. 139-140.

3. *Ibid.*

Chapter 15

✧✧✧✧✧✧✧

The Ineffective Pulpiteer's Family

I'd like to introduce you to a family of preachers not-to-be. These are folks who certainly feel called by God to deliver a good message when they preach but have either drifted into a pattern of bad habits in delivering sermons or have never had good speech training in preparation to be a preacher. Perhaps they have been good at one time but have developed in response to stage fright a number of distractions which sadly weakens the message they have to proclaim. Their edge in preaching has been dulled.

1. *Hot Foot Harriet.* She is enthusiastic, wants to be informal and is desperately trying to communicate something in which she believes deeply. However, she allows her nervousness to cause her to pace around the pulpit and in the chancel as she is speaking. It is very distracting to those who try to follow and listen to her.

2 *Thelma Thin Voice.* Some people are much more blessed with a voice that is resonant and contains timbre. Others will have to work their entire life to make their voices good public speaking and projecting voices. Thelma's voice is light and has very little timbre to it. In addition, she's never learned to abstain from eating dairy products before delivering a public speech. So when she comes under the pressure of standing before a congregation, the voice thinness is exacerbated and even more difficult and unpleasant to hear projected throughout the sanctuary.

3. *Victor Vocalized Pauses.* Here's a fellow who tries to be informal and deliver his sermon without notes or outline. While he's thinking what comes next, he's developed a very bad habit of saying "uhs" and "ahs" which don't mean a thing and terribly distract from communication.

4. *Walter Word Whiskers.* This preacher has a good vocabulary but he allows other phrases and words to come into his

communication. Such things as "you know" and "and things like that" have diluted the punch of the message.

5. *Fred Flitting Eyes.* Because of the pressure of being in front of the congregation, Fred never allows his eyes to get solid contact with any one person in the audience. He moves from his sermon notes out to the congregation and looks in general at them rather than any one specific person. His brother, *Alfred Above The Crowd,* was taught by someone to look just above the heads as he speaks. This is terrible advice. Alfred and Fred need to learn to look at their notes and then look up and concentrate on one face in one location, move to another face in another location, move to another face in another location, but staying with each long enough to allow real communication through the eye contact to take place.

6. *Rita Rocking-On-Pins.* A nervous habit has developed when Rita preaches as she rocks back on her heels and then up on her toes when making important points. While that feels pretty good to her, it gives a very humorous and odd appearance to those who watch her preach.

7. *Sarah Sentence-Trail.* The older members of the congregation who have some hearing impairment really get frustrated with Sarah. She has good things to say, is well prepared and says them with enthusiasm, but she allows the end of her sentences to trail off. I think there's another relative of hers, perhaps a cousin, who does just the opposite and talks "up." In other words, at the end of each sentence, her voice goes up and makes a very peculiar kind of speech pattern.

8. *Harvey Hero* or *Helen Heroine* are preachers who tell stories about their own ministries in their sermons and usually make themselves the center of the story, the wise person who saves the day. It certainly is important to include oneself in preaching but it does not go well with the congregation to make the preacher the hero or heroine.

9. *Bill Blurry Articulation.* Bill sometimes sounds like he has mush in his mouth. He has never learned the discipline of articulating each word carefully. One might say he has a lazy tongue. *Mumbling Mary* would be part of the same family. She isn't very confident of her ability to preach or the importance of

her message. So she mumbles it in a way that is almost unintelligible to understand. Perhaps both of these preachers have carried this habit from childhood forward. It may be a capitulation to lack of self-confidence or a rather shy personality. On the other hand, it just could be they haven't taken care of themselves and come to the pulpit tired and under a lot of external pressure.

10. *Max Monotone.* If there is a head of the ineffective pulpiteer's family or the oldest daughter or son, Max is probably it. He just lacks excitement in his sermon delivery. His sermons are almost always correct theologically but rarely does he communicate through his own enthusiasm and body language that they are very important to him or to those who hear him.

11. *Peter Petrified.* Peter's hands clamp on to the pulpit rail and never let go until the sermon's over. Once he gets into that pulpit and begins the message he is frozen in place. He really communicates to the congregation a cold and sterile, uninteresting gospel, not by what he says but by the way he looks. Peter Petrified is so frightened that he communicates the fear to the congregation and makes them very uneasy.

12. *Larry Lack-of-Focus.* Larry likes to cover many subjects in every sermon and throw into the content whatever he thinks of that week. He doesn't spend a lot of time on preparation to preach and so whatever he can think of that is clever or any stories that he recently heard he dumps into the content. When people go home and ask what the sermon is about, the usual answer is, "about fifteen minutes."

13. *Howard Holy Tone.* Howard believes that a different tone of voice ought to be used when we speak about God and when the preacher speaks on God's behalf. In regular conversation and other communication he's a very down-to-earth and rational person but when he gets into the pulpit and begins to preach, his words are extended and there's almost a vibrato in his voice that waves a bit like one of those electronic organs in a funeral home. It is so syrupy and remote from the world that children think of the pulpit being in heaven and the people on earth.

14. *Gary Glued-to-Manuscript.* Gary is confident that he can write out a better sermon word for word than he can preach

extemporaneously. Of course, Gary is correct. However, when the pressure of being in front of the congregation takes over, he sticks closely to his manuscript and the delightful playfulness of the spirit taking hold and surprising the preacher and congregation has been greatly diminished. Gary has great things prepared to say, even exciting things, but the eye contact is not there or it sounds so canned and memorized that the message just doesn't seem to have the integrity and spontaneity which is so important to healthy communication.

If you suspect you might belong to the "Ineffective Pulpiteer's Family," record your preaching on video tape and carefully review it after delivery. A spouse, speech teacher, or mature congregant, if asked, may be willing to critique your preaching for you after reading the above family traits.

Remember, no matter how well we win over the above delivery habits, they will come back again and again. We must be alert to their re-emergence for the rest of our preaching career. The pulpiteer's family genes are very strong and continue to reappear over and over again!

Chapter 16

❖❖❖❖❖❖❖

Wax Free Preaching

Sermons which use superlatives, trite, groping, repetitious, "and so forth" expressions still turn off congregational listeners.

Years ago in the speech department of Wittenberg College, Springfield, Ohio, Paul R. Brees warned me about these communication faults and required all his speech students to read Richard C. Borden's *Public Speaking, As Listeners Like It*, published 35 years ago. It was then and there I learned about wax in speeches and the need to remove it.

Congregations like sermons which are crisp, clear, and that reveal the Gospel rather than conceal it. That means with discipline we preachers must remove the wax from our preaching in order to keep our best edge in the proclamation.

We have all heard the illustration about Roman sculptors who used wax to cover the cracks and blemishes in their work. We have reminded our congregations how the word "sincere" comes from the custom of marking those statues which had no flaws filled with wax *sine cera*, literally, without wax.

Word-wax could be defined as any phrase or group of words which isn't an important part of the Gospel you seek to express in your sermon.

Consider the wax which Borden listed for platform speakers: superlatives, expressions which are trite, groping, repetitious, and . . . "and so forth." By careful removal of these habit-formed phrases and word-wax, your sermon will show real improvement.

Remove all *superlatives*. They are distracting and an inaccurate description of the real situation. We can restate "this was the most awe-inspiring and fantastic thing which ever happened to me" to a simple . . . "this moved me."

Congregational listeners have a way of doubting the truth of the description when the language is superlative and even more so when the preacher has a habit of using that kind of language often. They also tire of everything described as the best, biggest, and grandest. Get rid of the wax!

Trite phrases fill the message with useless verbiage and can dilute the punch and power of the Gospel we are called to proclaim. "A man who needs no introduction," "each and every man, woman, and child." Get rid of the stale and useless phrases that are like wax in the cracks of a genuine marble work of art.

Groping expressions weaken our veracity as preachers. When we qualify what we preach with statements like: "what I want to say is . . ." or "what I'm trying to get at is . . ." we communicate we are not all that sure of this Gospel ourselves. It sounds like the preacher wants to proclaim this great truth but fears he or she will be discovered wrong. So a groping phrase is added which admits the message isn't certain, precise and clear. Because we have a Gospel to preach, let's preach it without the wax of qualifiers and as confident witnesses to what we know to be true.

There's also the wax of *repetitious expressions.* "As I said before" or "may I repeat again" serves no purpose except to apologize to the listeners for having to fill the empty spots with repetition. While repetition is recommended in effective preaching, it does not help to call attention to the fact that you are repeating yourself.

"And so forth" expressions aren't any better than the rest of the above wax. They often sound to the listener as if the preacher wants them to believe that they know more than they really do.

"Just like the great reformers: Luther, Calvin, Wesley, Booth and so forth" sounds as if you could list many more but that may not be true. I heard a preacher say recently, "I can continue on this subject for hours." I wondered, really? With great depth and the wisdom of the ages as well, I suppose.

Weasel words are sermon wax, too. They will blur the possible crispness of the message and not only demonstrate a lack of confidence and certainty on the part of the preacher but encourage sloppy listening on the part of the hearer as well.

Remove the *punch-pulling phrases* from your sermons like: "perhaps this is only my opinion," "it might be true that . . . " and one that really levels out any certainty: "more or less."

Unlisted by Borden but mentioned by Paul R. Breese, my speech professor, and perhaps the thickest wax in our preaching, are the phrases that come from a desire to impress our listeners with our religiosity or simply to fill time until we can think what comes next. These are the *holy words* and *redundant theological terms* like, "Jesus Christ, Lord and Savior." Theological terms like eschatology, incarnation, existentialism, sanctification, and redemption are also good examples of intellectualizing.

Using genuine, close to the ground, simple vocabulary will help to communicate to a generation not raised in the church or schooled in theology and its shop talk.

	CLOSE TO THE GROUND SERMON LANGUAGE					
SERMON LANGUAGE	ACADEMIC	THEOLOGICAL	POLITE	PREACHER'S CULTURE	CLOSE TO THE GROUND	VULGAR,CRUDE,TABOO
	Bookish Pedantic Theoretical	God language Maudlin Pious	Third person Apologetic Couched	Ethnic Geographic Colloquial	Real Life Inclusive Sexual & Financial	Vernacular
An example describing DEATH:	career termination	escatological	deceased	passed away	died	"kicked the bucket" croaked

We can do better by cleaning out of our sermons this wax which makes the message uninteresting and unintelligible to our listeners. Let it be without redundant holy words, punch-pulling phrases, weasel words, repetitious expressions, and groping, trite and superlative phrases. Let it be close to the ground and without wax. Let it be sincere.

Chapter 17

✧✧✧✧✧✧✧

Sixteen Suggestions
For Good Preaching[1]

Martin Luther writes in his *Small Catechism* that the third article of the Apostles' Creed meant: "I believe that I cannot by my own reason or strength believe in Jesus Christ, my Lord, or come to Him; but the Holy Spirit has called me through the Gospel." So we, who are called to preach, proclaim while the Holy Spirit "calls" others through our preaching of that good gospel.

We must therefore ask ourselves some penetrating questions about our proclamation: Are we making the call clear in our preaching? Are we making that call of the Holy Spirit interesting and inviting? Are we using our own gifts of the Spirit in the best possible fashion in the pulpit? Are we creatively using well all the communication avenues open to us to proclaim the Gospel?

Here are sixteen suggestions for making our proclamation of the Gospel as clear and inspirational as possible. Try discussing them with a committee of lay people in your congregation and developing your edge as a preacher:

1. *Express the message as "good" news.* It's very easy to scold from the pulpit. However, in a day when self-esteem is low and self-worth is questioned, our message needs to build up people and to present Christ as a help today. We should tell our listeners that they have security in their practice of Christianity and that they are safe here and in eternity.

The law points out our need for the gospel, but law ought to be used sparingly. Don't forget God's grace. We must not forget to find gospel, the good news element, in all that we address from the pulpit.

There is a danger in what we call "triumphalism," which means that we simply talk about getting our soul saved for eternity and that "everything will be all right for us who believe." Because of a fear of this emphasis, we sometimes err in never bringing up those promises which are comforting and reassuring. We Christians are the community of the saved and do have glory from the cross to share. Let's remember that the "theology of the cross" is also hope-filled. When one beggar tells another beggar where to find food, it is with great delight that he/she tells of the nourishment and the discovery.

From the pulpit we have the privilege of affirming God's presence in the midst of the shambles of the lives of those who are gathered there.

Televangelists hold up for us a tantalizing ideal of positive thinking and smooth, thin, watered-down stuff which is far from the New Testament Gospel. Still, they have something we need to see as well. It is a message for present hope and a good news which assures, lifts up and encourages.

Consider the beatitudes of Jesus in Matthew 5. Some scholars think that these are his sermon themes. For the most part, they are congratulations on "how it is for a Christian now." So keep the message the Good News.

2. *Share yourself.* The word share is overused, but it describes best what we ought to be doing from the pulpit. People who listen to the proclamation of the Gospel need to see the proclaimer as human and warm, struggling with them. "Personal story can also enable preachers to enter the text and see both it and themselves from the inside. Here it is not a matter of raising questions and answering them. It is a matter of identifying with someone in the text and allowing that identification to run its course." [2]

As we write our sermons, we need to preach to ourselves, as well as to the congregation. These messages will often be our most effective proclamations. (If you always have wondered why rich people seem to get God's blessings and not you, say that, examine it, and let God's word guide you and your listeners.)

Be absolutely certain that your congregation has heard your "God story." Older clergy were taught in seminary that they should never use the "I" or relate their own life experiences. Still, when we look at the biblical heros, we find that they were willing to tell of their own experiences in order to instruct and inspire others.

Your congregation can relate to your spiritual struggles and especially will be interested about the way God has called you into your particular ministry and relationship with God.

3. *Be sure to announce the whole story — the heart of the Good News.* Preaching can sound very fragmented by using our church year calendar when we follow the lectionary. Try to place the text of your sermon in the larger plan of God to save us. After all, preaching is often re-announcing what we have heard many times before. But a person might have to attend church every Sunday for a full year in order to get the full Gospel story of what God has done for us.

In many of our congregations the cross, resurrection, and Spirit-with-us must be proclaimed every Sunday. A visitor may attend just one time and the preacher sinks or swims by that one particular proclamation.

Try occasionally giving a rather topical sermon, something like "From Moses to Luther in 20 Minutes," in which you give a summary of the Christian faith. However, guard against that proclamation's being so narrow and fragmented that it loses its significance for the first-time hearer or for those who are just beginning to mature in the faith.

4. *Be Bible obvious but not Bible idolatrous.* Textual preaching is essential and the people in our pews are hungry for it. A large segment of the congregational membership coming to our churches for worship wants to hear and see the Bible used even though it's not always for a good reason.

The scripture is what makes us unique and different: Christians are distinctive people. People flock to the pulpit where the Bible is central. Evangelist Billy Graham has set a good example for us of visually demonstrating from whence he reads as he holds that Bible up in front of himself.

In some congregations the worshipers can only guess what is on the pulpit desk: perhaps some distant typewritten manuscript. Try holding the Bible in your hands in sight of the congregation and reading the text from it. You'll find that this is a reassuring visual aid and will be appreciated by Christian laity.

5. *Preach from commitment for commitment.* Often we are tempted to exclude from our sermon the "so what?" We need to ask for an obvious change in response to our preaching. We need to be certain that we extend an invitation for people to take some action because of the Good News they have heard. Tell your people what that change should be. Answer the questions, "What does this truth have to do with me now?" "How should my work, play, life, daily ministry and congregational activity be affected by the truth which is proclaimed today from the pulpit?"

Remember that all who are seated in the pews may not be converted Christians. Explain the next step to take in order to move toward membership in the fellowship of believers and discipleship of Christ.

6. *Make the message inclusive.* Be sure, when "driving the message home" and describing what action needs to be taken because of this gospel, that you include all ages, sexes, and persons of color and ethnic backgrounds. Use heroes and heroines from other groupings as your examples.

This is also an opportunity for us to remove all sexist language from our vocabulary. It can be done gradually over a period of time and will be stimulating to the hearers of your proclamation.

Confess your concern about the congregation's make-up if it does not reflect the neighborhood. Don't scold. Love the people and confess your own frustration at trying to accomplish apostolic inclusiveness by making the congregation reflect the full richness of God's creation. Coax, encourage, love — and let the Spirit enlighten. (See chapter 10, "Preaching On Controversial Subjects.")

7. *Keep it simple.* In introducing country western singer Willie Nelson on a country music awards television program, the host said that Willie sang his music "close to the ground." Just as Willie sings simply of life's everyday occurrences, we need to proclaim our gospel "close to the ground" as well.

Remove the theological words that only a few can comprehend. Martin Luther writes:

> *In the pulpit we are to lay bare the breast and nourish*
> *the people with milk because every day a new church is*

raised up ... therefore just preach the catechism faithfully and distribute the milk. Complicated thoughts and issues we should discuss in private with the eggheads (Kluglingen). I don't think of Dr. Pomeranius, Jonas, or Philip in my sermons. They know more about it than I do. So I don't preach to them. I just preach to Hansie and Betsy.[3]

In our proclamation let's learn to use narratives which can be told easily and retold without reading from our notes.

And let's have a focus to what we proclaim. There should be an easily remembered theme which runs through the entire message. Although it should be in contemporary language it should not be faddish.

Much of our preaching, if it's to be "close to the ground," will come from our experiences in giving pastoral care while making home visits and hospital calls the week before.

If you can find a related object which can be held up for your listeners to see, it will provide additional focus and stimulate their ability to remember what has been said.

8. *Let it be well illustrated.* Be sure that you use "windows" in the sermon such as stories, anecdotes, and good humor which will portray the great truths you want to proclaim. Have more examples ready than you'll need so that they can be used when you feel the need for more illustrative material.

Let the examples be yours! Carry a notepad with you all week so that you can write down things as you see them happen. Try to keep away from the books of illustrations which often use the life of Napoleon, Lincoln, and Joan of Arc! It's better to use your daily newspapers and news magazines which are full of stories illustrative of the struggles which we humans face. Develop a file of these under general headings.

There is good reason for knowing the theme and text of the day ahead of time: so that incidents will ring a bell as you observe them. Be sure to watch television, see contemporary movies, go to sports events, and generally live "close to the ground," as your congregation does, so that your illustrative material is real and meaningful to them.

9. *Tell the people ahead of time what to prepare for in the proclamation.* Often an introduction to the sermon theme and a brief outline can be included in the worship bulletin. If you have a weekly newsletter, an item can be placed there as well under the title, "Get Ready for Worship."

Use banners, inserts, and children's sermons to help drive home this focus of the day.

A congregation will be very appreciative if you will step out into the sanctuary before the worship service begins and briefly describe the theme for the worship service and what you'll be trying to accomplish in the sermon. You may also want to point out in the scripture lessons, prayers, and hymn of the day how that theme is further revealed.

The anticipation of following this theme adds a great deal in making communication effective as you actually do it.

10. *Keep it short.* Our present generation has been brought up on fourteen to fifteen minute segments on television and are conditioned to short attention requirements. I doubt if it is productive to preach, no matter how eloquent we are, more than fifteen minutes — twelve is probably better. If we do go for the longer sermon, we must make absolutely certain that we have a "change of pace" in order to attack the message in a different fashion to give variety and accommodate the short attention spans of these folks to whom we proclaim in our day.

A four or five minute children's sermon using a good visual aid and a fifteen minute adult sermon on the same theme will do more than twenty minutes of theological eloquence! However, it probably is true that children's sermons which are most effective are usually given by people for whom that comes very naturally. If that's not our thing to do, we probably shouldn't try.

11. *Involve lay people in proclamation and evaluation.* Several times a year be sure to ask your congregation what subjects they would like dealt with from the pulpit. Reuel Howe writes:

> *The minister preaches his sermon in order that other sermons may be brought into being in the congregation, sermons that will be the joint products of both his and*

110

the congregation's effort. This sermon which is the church's sermon, the joint product of the preacher's message — the congregation's meanings expressed through their listening.[4]

Ask the worship committee to help with sermon planning by providing a worship survey. Be sure to ask people who are not attending church as well as those who are regularly present each week.

Many congregations find it valuable to have a discussion of the sermon immediately after the service in some kind of informal format, perhaps over coffee. "People sermons" are well received by congregations. Ask seven or eight members of the congregation from various backgrounds, cultures and ages to come together with you on a Tuesday night to study the scripture for the following Sunday and share their ideas of what God would like to have proclaimed from the pulpit because of that scripture. Write down as many of the comments as possible. Then, as you work at preparing your sermon during the rest of the week, make a conscious effort to quote these folks by name (if you have their permission) in the sermon itself. You will find this an exciting way to communicate the message and downright fun for the people who help you, those who hear you, and yourself. Don't neglect to get together with the assisting group for Sunday lunch and talk about how it went.

Using preaching partners is another magnificent way to stimulate your proclamation of the gospel. For six months enlist a half-dozen people who will fill out an information sheet each week concerning their thoughts about the scripture and return the paper to the church by the Tuesday or Wednesday prior to your preaching the sermon. This sheet can ask the preaching partner to give a number of suggestions as follows:

PREACHING PARTNERS HELP

For Sunday: _____ Date: _____

Gospel:_____ O.T. Lesson:_____

Here is how the text affects me:_____

_____

Questions I would like answered about this scripture:_____

_____

Here is what I think God would want said to our congregation

Sunday:_____

_____

Illustrations I think of:_____

_____

Ideas from my journal:_____

_____

Newspaper, TV, movie, magazine ideas:_____

_____

Some ideas I suggest for our church because of this gospel:_____

_____

Signed_____

Your Preaching Partner

Return to the pastor before noon each Wednesday.

12. *Get excited and have enthusiasm.* It seems to me that people "catch the gospel" like they catch the measles rather than intellectually internalizing it.

If our rescue is that great and the news is that grand, why not let it become contagious in our presentation?

> *Our homilies are rarely heretical. They fail, fall short, founder rather because they are stale and flat, vapid and insipid, dreadfully dry and boringly barren. One reason? They are not pregnant with the inexhaustible riches that is Christ; they carry so little substance, so little sap to slack the parched spirit.*[5]

If that is true then the preacher cannot be bound to a manuscript or always fenced in with a pulpit. Let the hands be free for meaningful gestures! Diligently guard against that holy tone, laughingly called "stained glass voice," which often invades our speech when we get inside that pulpit.

It helps to keep a critic watching you for "word whiskers," "verbal pauses," and mannerisms described in chapters 15 and 16 which individual members of the congregation will notice but will not tell you.

Most dynamic preachers claim that they cannot deliver a good sermon unless it has been practiced out loud ahead of time! The same is also true of reading the scripture in a meaningful fashion. It is important to do in order to keep our preaching edge.

13. *Vary it — change the way it's presented.* It is just not reasonable any longer to give "three points and a poem" and call it stimulating proclamation. Our competition with electronic communication is real: it is professional, effective and to the point. We can do it well also because of our God-given preacher's edge.

As a result, we need to find as many ways to vary the proclamation as possible. The following is a list of some variations which can be considered:
- sermon dramas
- teaching sermons
- dialogue sermons

•Bible studies
•several voices reading scripture
•people sermons
•use of visual aids
•outline of the sermon in the bulletin
•a sermon series on a common theme
•a hymn in the middle
•lay people offering several prayers throughout the sermon

14. *Deal with issues of the day.* Although some pastors are fearful of dealing with controversial issues, this type of sermon subject doesn't need to offend. We should not be afraid to take on the tough issues that everyone is thinking about anyway. (See chapter 10, "Preaching On Controversial Subjects.")

> *I do not see how you can bar the controversial from the pulpit simply because it is controversial. After all, I cannot be content with glittering generalities; I must move the Gospel to this age, to this people; but the meaning and demands of the Gospel today are chock full of complexity. And the more complex an issue, the more open to controversy.*[6]

If the preacher holds up the general biblical truths alongside the problem and admits that he or she, too, struggles and is even frightened to present it to the congregation, it helps the listeners to identify with the struggle and think more about the issue itself.

One must avoid presenting the gospel in such a fashion on social justice issues that if individuals don't agree with you, they feel you're saying they're going to hell. We haven't accomplished anything constructive if we drive away those people whose minds need to be opened for inspiration and change. Instead, they must be called to discipleship through our proclamation. A congregation will respect the preacher who does not scold but coaxes, encourages and stimulates further discussion.

15. *Be sure to talk about money.* Money is what Americans understand best. It directs our lives. How we get it, what we do with it, and how we give it away are very big issues and often set all the rest of our priorities.

To be relevant we must talk about our cash, credit cards, savings accounts, charge accounts, and investments. In this country a person's checkbook is still the best indicator of who that person is and what he or she worships. Certainly we have missed touching a large part of our parishioners' lives if we ignore the subject of money.

16. *Take seriously the Holy Spirit.* While this is last in the list, it is by far the most important! So much of the rest of the worship is cut and dried, in print and predictable. But during these fifteen minutes of preaching we can allow for the surprises, mystery, and playfulness — the serendipity — to take place.

In *Black Preaching*, we read

> *The term hermeneutic is most fittingly applied to this process of spiritual growth. A preacher who does not have this capacity flirts with boredom and loss of attention. Black worshippers want to be stirred; they want to have an emotional experience. But they also want to be stretched, helped, and fed. They want the cream of the Black pulpit — the kind of preaching that is highly relevant in content and charismatic in delivery.*[7]

All week get the text in mind and let yourself be inspired by God's Spirit. Allow the text to direct your own life as well. Then pray before you go into that pulpit — and lay yourself open so that God can come into you and surprise even you. By the time you get into the pulpit, if properly prepared, preaching will be from the overflow, and your edge will be obvious.

Walter J. Burghardt writes:

> *What I am commending to the preacher is a spirituality that is biblically based — and especially so. Not simply the study of Old Testament and New Testament spirituality, though this can base the broader life of the spirit. Rather, a reverent immersion in Scripture such that intelligence is subservient to love.*[8]

115

Never apologize by saying, "I'm no theologian" or "I'm not a great preacher." It's God's good news we bear. It's God's Spirit that is aching to be set free through us.

Prayer is the center. We Christians need to take seriously our beliefs about that Spirit and learn how to open up our lives to her so that she can speak through us.

Hear the words of John Burke in *Gospel Power:* "The good news of salvation needs to be spelled out in words that excite the imagination, inform the mind and inflame the heart . . . the preacher's own faith compels speech which, in its turn, gives birth to faith in the listener. Faith speaks to faith."[9]

Let's remind ourselves as we approach the pulpit, "I cannot by my own reason or strength believe in Jesus Christ, my Lord, or come to Him; but the Holy Spirit has called me by the gospel." — Martin Luther's *Small Catechism*

1. From Jerry Schmalenberger, *Called to Witness* (Lima, Ohio: CSS Publishing Co. Inc., 1993).

2. Richard L. Thulin, *The "I" of the Sermon* (Philadelphia: Fortress Press, 1986), p. 49.

3. Fred W. Meuser, *Luther, The Preacher* (Minneapolis: Augsburg Press, 1973), p. 53.

4. Reuel L. Howe, *Partners In Preaching* (New York: Seabury Press, 1967), p. 31.

5. Walter J. Burghardt, S.J., *Preaching: The Art and the Craft* (New York: Paulist Press, 1987), p. 87.

6. *Ibid.*, p. 135.

7. Henry H. Mitchell, *Black Preaching, The Recovery of a Powerful Art* (Nashville: Abingdon Press, 1990), p. 103.

8. Burghardt, p. 87.

9. John Burke, *Gospel Power* (New York: P.O. Alba House, 1978), p. 4.

✧✧✧✧✧✧✧

Chapter 18

Reformation For These Days

All Saints' Lutheran Church, Worthington, Ohio
Reformation Sunday

Sermon move: Build A Fire
In these hands I held the very Bible Martin Luther used years ago to prepare his sermons. On the page which contained John 8, which I just read to you, he had scrawled the German words for "free indeed!"

Martin Luther was born in Eisleben, Germany, and never returned to the little village until he went back to settle an argument between two dukes and died there. I have often travelled to Eisleben to escort tour groups and to see the actual Reformation places. On one of those trips, the sexton of the church across the street from where Luther preached his last sermon offered to take me to the bell tower. We climbed up those steps and I was surprised to discover that the Lutherans from Wittenberg had moved the personal library of Martin Luther and some of the furniture from his study into a room high in that bell tower of the church. They kept it a secret it was there because they did not want the Communist regime which ran the country at the time to know about it.

In that room I was able to pick up with these hands the very Bible from which Luther prepared his sermons in the later years of his ministry. I read with my own eyes those German words scrawled in the margin of John 8, "free indeed!"

Sermon move: Build A Bridge
You have come to church today — and it's Reformation Sunday. It is the Sunday before All Saints' Day and October 31, when Luther nailed his thesis on the doors of the castle church in Wittenberg,

Germany, which began the Protestant Reformation. But that was so far from here and it was so long ago.

You are probably wondering what the Reformation of the sixteenth century can say to you which is important to your life at the dawning of the twenty-first century here in Worthington, Ohio, in this year of 1994? In a day of information highways, satellite uplink and downlinks, compressed digital signals, and other advanced technology, perhaps you're wondering if anything would apply from back then right now for you.

Besides, we Lutherans don't hate Catholics anymore, our Bibles haven't been chained to the wall for a long time, pastors can and do marry, and I don't think indulgences are being sold in any of our congregations.

But if you're struggling today with a weighty problem that hangs heavy on your heart, if you're fighting an addiction, if you're eager for something deeper spiritually, if you need some of God's shalom in your hectic and frantic life, if you're desperate for forgiveness, if you would like to see more significance in your job, perhaps Reformation Sunday is just what you're looking for.

Sermon move: The Point
You see, this day of Reformation has a lot to say to us who have gathered here to celebrate our heritage: In Christ, there is freedom for us.

Sermon move: The Example
Martin Luther's strong emphasis on the value of the scripture still equips us for life in the 1990s — for therein is truth and. . . "truth sets us free."

Listen to what the Gospel of John reports Jesus saying: "To the Jews who believed in him Jesus said: 'If you make my word your home you will indeed be my disciples; you will come to know the truth and the truth will set you free' " (John 8:31-32 TJB).

So from the scripture we have a promise we can count on: "If you make my word your home you will indeed be my disciples; and you will come to know the truth."

For a day when we talk a lot about getting even — Jesus says to turn the other cheek . . . that's the truth of it!

For a day when we are taught to get what's coming to us, stake out our own turf, demand our rights — Jesus teaches us that it is more blessed to give than it is to receive . . . that's the truth of it! For a time when we are advised to ignore the misfits, immigrants, welfare recipients, the freeloaders — Jesus teaches us to love those who will never love us or thank us back and that's the truth of it.

In a time when we are in serious danger of being a slave to wealth addiction, our sexual desires, self-centeredness, our own ego needs, power over others, Jesus says the truth is that there is a life of discipleship which frees us to be a different kind of human being. No longer are we paralyzed by guilt and shame, no longer are we afraid of being alone or of facing a terminal illness or even death, no longer need we doubt that we have God's forgiveness because we have not lived a good enough life. We are set free. We can have God's love even though we don't deserve it.

Luther didn't invent a new church. What he did was point us again to a church of the New Testament and Pentecost when humans were just as sinful and the church as imperfect as it is right now. Whenever we lose the marks of the church of Pentecost: an experience of the alive Christ, a passion to witness to our faith, an unbreakable fellowship with the changed group, a love of people, an inward security or peace, and a deep sense of joy, we need Martin Luthers. They must point us once more to the wonderful undeserved grace of God which sets us free to be God's people called the church.

Luther also took the idea of ministry away from a few ordained clergy and placed it right in the laps of every baptized person. One of the slogans of our foremothers and forefathers who fought that sixteenth century Reformation was "the priesthood of all believers." That's the truth of it!

This was, and is, radical stuff! In our baptism we believe we are called to be ministers and do ministry every day where we work, live, and play. That's the meaning of Christian vocation. We identify our gifts, skills, and abilities and then find ways to use them to do ministry every day of the week.

Look how that changes our attitude toward worship. Now it becomes the time when all the ministers report in and get a word of advice, encouragement, and help from each other.

Look how that changes our attitude toward our job. Now we don't see it as just a way to earn a certain amount of money. We see it as an opportunity to witness to our faith and to minister to the other people we work beside.

Look how that changes our attitude toward marriage and parenting. We begin to see our children as a treasure over which we are stewards for a brief period of time. We begin to see our spouse not as someone who needs to satisfy us but rather as a person who has forgiveness and the opportunity to start over again and again, too.

Students going to school see their opportunities to learn more than a drudgery. It becomes the possibility of reaching their full creative potential that God would have them reach.

Think how that changes our attitude toward our retirement years. Rather than seen as a time when we withdraw and say let the younger generation do it, we see it as a time when we can carry out a special ministry of love and compassion to others. We can see these all as opportunities to which God has called us to be ministers. So we can see Reformation has a lot to say to us today about how and when and where we live.

Sermon move: Preacher's Witness

It really means a lot to me to be Lutheran and Christian and part of a reforming church. I grew up in St. Paul's Lutheran Church in Greenville, Ohio, not too many miles west of here. Oh, how I learned from Reverend Wessel, my pastor, about the free gift of God's grace in that little German congregation. On the day I was examined for confirmation in front of the congregation I had memorized the answer to every seventh question that we knew Reverend Wessel was going to address to us. But one of the confirmands did not show up! That threw the rotation off after the first question. Nevertheless, that sainted pastor said yes to my answers even though they didn't fit the question at all. What grace I learned from him that day!

I see all around me where I live in California, in my family, among my friends, on my travels around the world, a hunger still to know that wonderful, radical amazing grace of God which wants so much to bring healing to relationships. It's a grace which wants forgiveness for transgressions and wants the possibility for us to start anew every day.

I see that promise to lighten the load as needed now as much as it was when Jesus first promised it and Luther called attention to it again.

I also need the joy which is available from being one of God's disciples. It's a joy that's more than the opposite of unhappy; it's a joy that's the opposite of unbelief. It's a joy that comes not from the absence of trouble in my life, but rather the presence of God.

I'm absolutely certain there is a message today, Reformation Sunday, for me. I'm delighted to be a Lutheran and a son of the Reformation, with a strong belief about a God who forgives when we don't deserve it; a God who calls us through our baptisms to do ministry in the world; a God who gives to us the Bible that life might be better directed, easier, fuller, wiser and of great joy.

Sermon move: So What? Action Steps

Let me challenge you this Sunday of Reformation to a Reformation of your own religious life as well. Try this:

1. Start a daily reading of the Bible. If only for ten minutes, get started on it. Begin with the gospel of Matthew in the New Testament and then move from there to the Acts of the Apostles.

2. Take a new look at your vocation, your job. Do something this week that ministers to someone else at work and try it in your own home as well. See yourself as servant rather than demanding what's coming to you.

3. Tell someone quietly what your faith means to you. Tell them how God's grace is for them also. The wonderful thing about witnessing to your faith is each time you tell it to someone else you own it more yourself. And the more you own it the better you tell it. What a wonderful way it works for us in our faith.

Sermon move: Finish Up/Frame

It was a thrill to hold Luther's Bible in my own hands there in the bell tower of the old church in Eisleben, Germany, across the street from where Luther died. "Free indeed" he wrote across the page of John 8. But even greater than that thrill is the fact that we now hold in our heart what Luther underlined in John's gospel: "If you make my word your home you will indeed be my disciples; you will come to know the truth and the truth will set you free" (John 8:31-32).

Free indeed!

Amen.

Chapter 19

✧✧✧✧✧✧✧

Judah's Song Of Victory
(An Extended Narrative Sample Sermon)
(Isaiah 26)

The Story Begins
The San Francisco Chronicle headed the story like this, "Garage Sale Yields Trove of Autographs." Dr. Scott Kinnes was a critical care specialist in Hawaii until he went to a garage sale not far from his home on a Sunday morning last year.

An elderly woman in his neighborhood was selling stuff out of her garage and Scott decided he would rummage through it. He found a row of black trash bags stuffed with old papers and photos of movie stars. Upon examining them carefully, he found that the photographs were signed and they had been obtained by the Zanes sisters who worked at the San Francisco Opera House and the Curran Theatre. Clark Gable, Charlie Chaplin, Laurel and Hardy, Mary Pickford, Vivian Leigh, and Carole Lombard were a few of the many discovered. There were also pictures of a number of the presidents of the United States, autographed!

The lady who was holding the rummage sale was the older sister of the two Zanes sisters who were deceased. She said she wanted to be rid of the stuff that had been gathered over more than forty years. That "stuff" has now been appraised as being worth more than one million dollars!

Transition to the Scripture
I'd like to hold a garage sale here for you and rummage through some of the old theological pictures and signed bags of stuff that might be treasures for us even this day. Isaiah has God promising, "Those of steadfast mind you keep in peace — in peace because they trust in you." And verse 12: "O Lord, you will ordain peace for us . . . " (Isaiah 26:3, 12, NRSV). Let's open some bags.

So to a hectic world we have the gift of peace to offer. To those who are struggling desperately to keep their marriages together; the single parent who wants to do it well and is having a terrible time; the person out of job and money; the one addicted to drugs; the other sexually out of control and full of guilt; still others who are afraid of terminal illness gnawing inside their bodies; or the person left all alone who is terribly frightened by old age. To these folks we can open the bag of peace.

Some Illustration
To lifestyles which are frenetic, frenzied, frantic, frustrated, and fragmented, we have peace.

Yesterday on CNN airport network they flashed what they called a "factoid" across the screen: "Forty-four per cent of our population says their families frequently cause them stress." That's not new news to any parish pastor or any person who has lived in family! For them we have peace.

Humor for Relief
Not very long ago in the pre-trials for Olympic ice-skating, one of the contenders lost her balance, fell, slid across the ice and into the judges' bench. She knocked the judges onto the floor in a heap. They gradually righted themselves and held up their scorecards for her performance: one, zero, zero, two, zero, *nine*. They all turned to the judge who had given the nine and asked why he would do so. His answer was simple: "I know it's slippery as hell out there!" To those people out there where life is "slippery as hell" we can offer peace. To those in family stress we can open the bag of peace as well.

It's been there all along — it's part of being one of God's own people. It's our bag just like the Zanes sisters and we can open it wide and spread it around. "You keep in peace . . . you will ordain peace for us. . . ."

Metaphoric Language
There is a certain freedom that we have in being God's people and that must be in the bag as well. Verse 13 (NRSV) says: "O

124

Lord our God, other lords besides you have ruled over us . . ." and so they have, over us as well! The god of prestige, selfishness, pride, self-indulgence; the god of wealth addiction and power addiction we worship. To a time and culture that demand their rights and privileges and that do anything to get what's coming to them, we have a Lord we can turn to who sets us free from the world's lords. We have as our bag and those to whom we witness: bags of freedom.

It's All Saints' Sunday and we can proclaim and own for ourselves a freedom from the dread of death as well. We have a freedom from the slavery of sacrificing family, spouses, health, friendship, in order to own things once thought luxuries but now considered essential.

Narrative Extended

I think it's interesting that Scott Kinnes quit his job after discovering that treasure trove worth a million dollars. I wonder how happy he is a year later?

You and I can open this bag, find the treasure like Scott Kinnes did. Judah's people sang what we can sing: "O Lord our God, other lords besides you have ruled over us. . . ." But not now — we are set free.

We also have an enormous bag full of undeserved love that's available to us. "Your dead shall live, their corpses shall rise" (v. 19, NRSV).

Metaphor Extended

What was worthless and unimportant now lives anew — the bags of autographed photos have new life, thanks to Scott Kinnes. Thanks to the Christ who came to be our Immanuel, that is, God with us. That Christ went to the cross that we might have forgiveness, came out of the grave that we might also have resurrection, and returned in spirit to equip us to live to the fullest right now.

We can be sure of our eternity because of his undeserved love for us.

A New Narrative Current Event — Probably Not Needed

American Eagle 4184 crashed in a soybean field just short of O'Hare Field's runway last week. You and I have the only bag worthwhile to those who died on that flight and to those who grieve them. It's the only dance they can dance out there in that bean field: "Your dead shall live, their corpses shall rise."

To be loved like that and to love like that is a marvelous thing. Open that bag for yourself and those you witness to.

Forgiveness for our guilt is in the bag for us too. We need not carry a load of baggage from the past that burdens us down in the future. We can unpack the bag in God's presence and be done with it.

Current Event

Susan Smith of Union, South Carolina, allegedly murdered her sons Michael and Alex. She claimed that a black carjacker had taken her car and the kids. The whole community stood behind her as she lied about it until it was discovered that she had strapped them in the back seat of her car and drowned them in a nearby lake.

"I've been standing by this girl through thick and thin. I've never doubted her," said a tearful Susan Pugram. "The children are really okay now. They are in the hands of God." Susan Pugram knows the wonderful forgiveness God has worked for all of us.

She knows it won't be the "Mickey Mouse flowers" in the casket that will save those children but rather a God who forgives.

Another citizen of the community is quoted as saying: "What they should do is turn her over to us. We would do to her the same as she did to her children." That person has a long way yet to go to understand the radical nature of God's forgiveness and how that same God would have us forgive each other. It's in our bag.

Narrative Continues

Like the Zanes sisters we have the picture of Christ on the cross. And his Good Friday signature is on it. In his name we pray and live our discipleship. At the time they gathered those pictures, they were so precious to them. But evidently the sisters had forgotten what a treasure they had. Or perhaps they simply hadn't told anyone else about their treasure.

Metaphoric Language

We have the same situation, too. A whole treasure trove of forgiveness, unconditional love, freedom, and peace. It is worth a fortune to us now and here.

Here's a bag I really enjoy. It's called the real presence of Christ. In verse 9 of Judah's Song of Victory we read: "My soul yearns for you in the night, my spirit within me earnestly seeks you."

Open the bag of Holy Spirit now. When we Christians take the holy communion we believe in the real presence of Christ in that bread and wine. We are sustained by it over and over again. Martin Luther, the great reformer and preacher, also taught about the real presence of Christ in preaching. He believed that in the sermon one actually encounters God. Over and over the autographed picture comes alive and is with us in spirit.

We have a generation out there that wants to be put in touch with the supernatural, as they call it. We can do that. It's our bag. When we preach, teach, give out the sacrament of communion, worship, receive the bread and wine, it's like Kellogg's Corn Flakes wants it to be: "Taste them again for the first time."

"O dwellers in the dust, awake and sing for joy" (v. 19b).

Ours is not a grim duty but a marvelous privilege. And we must open and reopen that bag many times. Let our song be a joy-filled song. In Matthew 5 Jesus is recorded as listing out the congratulations of being a disciple and Christian. He lists for us in those beatitudes how joy is found in following God. Let's open wide that bag this All Saints' Sunday and celebrate.

There is a joy when we are completely dependent on God.

Even when we grieve and mourn there is a joy to be found.

There is a joy for us when we keep our sinful selves under control.

We have satisfaction as we seek the holy.

We will be treated mercifully as we treat others hat way.
God's Spirit will bring purity to our hearts.
As we share the shalom we become daughters and sons of God.

And even when we take it on the chin for our discipleship, we will taste a portion of the kingdom. Now that's a bag full and overflowing with joy, joy, joy.

The Frame — Return to Beginning

When Dr. Scott Kinnes began his walk on Sunday morning and strolled into that garage sale, I'm confident he never dreamed that he would find such treasures in those trash bags. Personally autographed pictures of people like Duke Ellington, Orson Welles, and Errol Flynn. But then too, when we casually stroll into church and our pulpits, perhaps we don't imagine or expect such life-changing treasures either.

Summary in Reverse Order

We have then available:
Great joy.
Christ's real presence.
Precious forgiveness.
Undeserved radical love.
Freedom from the world's slavery and God's blessed peace.
It's all in Judah's Song of Victory recorded in Isaiah 26.

A Kicker!

And as far as this sermon goes, well — it's in the bag!
Amen.

Chapter 20

❖❖❖❖❖❖❖

Belle Plaine's Gusher
(A Local History Sample Sermon)

It all started when the village of Belle Plaine hired William Wier for $350 to dig a well for the city and the south side's schoolhouse. On August 26, 1886, at 1:30 p.m., the well-digger struck water at 193 feet. The next day he returned to find a large amount of water belching into the air. The well increased in size all that day. The flow enlarged to one-and-a-half-feet wide, spurting eight feet into the air. William Wier quietly left town.

The water spout, dubbed "Jumbo," got larger and larger. The citizens of the little town were excited, then frantic, and almost crazy. The two-inch hole was now expanded to three feet in diameter, as rocks and sand roared from its gaping mouth. The City Council couldn't get Jumbo shut off. Months went by, and two streams over twelve feet wide developed to carry the water to the Iowa River.

Of course, the press traveled to Belle Plaine from all over and terribly exaggerated the well's size and effect. Sketches were drawn and published of rescuing Belle Plaine's citizens from second-floor windows! It was described in distant newspapers as "water spouting hundreds of feet into the air with a roar that could be heard from miles around."[1]

Soon people claimed magical cures performed by drinking its water. They tried a lot of different ways to stop the tremendous flow of water, but to no avail. A man from Marshalltown by the name of Luther King was hired for $2,000 to cap the now-famous artesian gusher. He started to build a high wooden fence around it, and charged spectators to get in and see the strange fountain of Belle Plaine. Finally, as a last resort, the Council engaged the services of a local foundry, Palmer Brothers. On October 16, 1887, thirteen months after the well was opened, it was closed with hydraulic jacks and great quantities of sand and cement. An asphalt road now covers the place where Jumbo gushed forth.

Before they got the geyser quieted down, there had been dumped into its gaping mouth 200 feet of pipe, 40 carloads of stone, and 130 barrels of cement.

It's an unusual story of a well that went berserk and showed a whole community the latent power of water that lay just 200 feet below its surface. I call it the "Parable of Belle Plaine's Gusher." It's one of Iowa's greatest.

I'm rather sure that William Wier, contractor King from Marshalltown, and the City Council would not agree, but God's grace is like this artesian well of Belle Plaine — free and plentiful!

God's grace comes without effort on our part — it's God's gift and usually a surprise. Grace means "gift" — it is central to our Christian belief that God's love for us, God's saving action, God's help in our suffering and trouble, is all a gift. It just pours out to us like "Jumbo" of Belle Plaine.

Saint Paul writes, "All who receive God's *abundant* grace and are freely put right with him will rule in life through Christ" (Romans 5:17b, GNB).

When we kneel for Communion, when we are adopted by Baptism, that life-giving and death-protecting gift of grace was, and is, God's gift to us. It is not deserved; it is not earned or even expected. Dr. Joseph Sittler, Lutheran theologian, said of infant baptism: "It's a recognition that we weren't consulted in the first place."

It's no accident we use water when we baptize with God's grace. We even call the baptismal container a "font." "Font" comes from "fountain" and, much like Belle Plaine's gusher, from this well of grace God comes with many blessings.

God's grace doesn't run out either! Scripture assures us God's love and grace are all-sufficient. They don't run out, wear out, or dribble away for lack of supply. The hymn "There's A Wideness In God's Mercy" assures us, "There is grace enough for thousands . . . ."

We may have come to God's grace-well many times before, but we are always welcome to return for more. There is no rationing; you don't have to have shirt and shoes to get it either.

We may have resolved the last time we received God's grace, we would do better and be better, and here we are again at the table and before the altar. God loves; God's still here with the gift of forgiveness.

It surprises us when and where we least expect it. Old William Wier got a surprise when he returned the next day. Boy, did he have a well! God surprises us, too — amazing grace spurts forth at some of the most peculiar times:

- when someone dies,
- at the birth of a child,
- during the singing of a hymn,
- when we grow bitter at someone else,
- at the hospital bed,
- when we have strayed and guilt burns in our bellies,
- in visiting a neighbor,
- in loving a spouse,
- in the loneliness of the late night,
- before the humdrum and routine meal.

God gives grace, and we are blessed and surprised.

And like the gusher of Belle Plaine, grace is available to everyone. No one can build a fence around it, even though they try. Like a fresh and lovely lagoon in a public park, all can gather around and be cooled, comforted, washed, and inspired. Like a public drinking fountain in the center of town, all can come and have their thirst quenched. There are no restrictions, no requirements, no superficial barriers. Race, sex, educational status, color, nationality — these make no difference. God's grace is for all.

The more we receive, the more there is available to us. That's right — like "Jumbo" which got larger and larger, once we accept and receive God's gift of amazing grace, it just opens up to us more and more.

The water in the Belle Plaine gusher was tested by the Chicago and Northwestern Railroad Company. It was found to be unsuitable for use in locomotives, and word was spread not to drink it. Nevertheless people did, and before long the word was out it could heal. A Mr. J. Baker wrote, "For 30 years I have suffered with dyspepsia and its concomitant troubles, and suffered much from nervous exhaustion. The use of the Belle Plaine Mineral Water has greatly benefited me. Have not been so well in ten years." God's grace — God's will — is healing, too. In fact, we describe health and "being all right" with the word "well." Come to this well where you are given a gift of love and forgiveness and healing can take place. Not only for troubled and distraught minds, but for difficulty in the marriage, strife with the parents and kids, and other human relationships which are tearing you apart. When we let God's grace work in our own lives, healing can take place where we have hurt each other. And healing, too, can happen when our physical being has disintegrated because of worry, stress, guilt, and lack of self-worth.

God's grace is, indeed, like Belle Plaine's gusher, because it just pours out without our deserving, and all we need do is gather around and marvel at it.

As wonderful as this grace of God can be, there are those who would misuse it. Like Luther King who came from Marshalltown, who had a man go down into the well in a diving suit several times and built a fence around it in order to sell admissions, our use of God's free and abundant grace can be terribly commercial. Some would reduce the business of the Church to a commercial venture. All discussions can be made on the basis of profit and loss, rather than God's mission. We have a great well gushing forth, and our main job is to get that grace out to all who have need of it.

To take credit for our grand Church or ministry — for God's great blessings here — would be as silly as William Wier standing by the gusher, flexing his suspenders and bragging, "Look what I did!"

I think most of us are more like the driller when he quietly got out of town the next morning. That was more well than he wanted to take responsibility for! We behave in a similar fashion. We have an infant baptized and never come to worship again. We are confirmed on Pentecost and leave the fellowship of believers until marriage. We make all those religious vows before God's altar and then tell the spouse to do the church work. It's tempting to be like that frightened well driller and quietly leave town!

Let's remember Wier and King and how easy it is to misuse this wonderful grace.

God's grace remains untapped for most of us. If you go to the corner of 8th Avenue and 8th Street next to Charlie Stall's place in Belle Plaine today, there is only a paved street over all that hydraulic power and a piece of granite with a bronze plaque along the curb that marks the location of the phenomenon. It was placed there on December 3, 1954, by the Ladies of Artesia Chapter of The Daughters of the American Revolution. For a number of years, townspeople walked around the place, keeping their eyes on the spot, a little uneasy that it might erupt and gush forth again.

We tiptoe around our church in similar fashion — this place where there is so much grace power and where the well is abundant and plentiful.

If we ever set free all this which God would like to pour out into our congregation and into our community, what drastic changes could take place. Even more than an artesian well gone berserk, our witnessing to the forgiveness available and the love of one another and for enemies could baptize this congregation and community in a new spirit.

This baptismal water has that kind of power. But we often treat it so casually and drop a little moisture on the head of a child in a pious fashion. There is power in that font and grace in that water. Our worship service ought to be like dancing and playing in and around that water, much like children do in and through a lawn sprinkler on a hot day in Iowa.

In January of 1957, on the Elmer Jones farm southeast of Belle Plaine, a well was drilled. After it was capped, water worked its way outside of the casing and the cap had to be removed. Six tons of crushed rock were used to stop the flow. Three weeks later, the well broke loose again. The pressure lost caused other wells in the area to slow or cease. The well was finally recased and ceased being troublesome. At the writing of this sermon, no other "gushers" have broken loose, but the possibility is ever present around Belle Plaine. There is power just below the surface there . . . and it's here, too.

133

The cross of Jesus Christ is a lot like Belle Plaine's "Jumbo." In it is power and it gives to us unexpected and undeserved water of life: a chance to start over, a sense of self-worth, life after this earthly one, a way to love the unlovely, His Spirit with us here, a new and good relationship with our God.

What a story — a well that just couldn't be stopped! It's an Iowa parable about how God gives to us in a surprising and so very generous way. It tells us:

> For so many, God's grace remains untapped.
> God's grace can be terribly misused.
> His grace is like an artesian well — free and plenty.
> It comes to us on its own.

"It is by God's grace that you have been saved . . . He did this to demonstrate for all time to come the extraordinary greatness of his grace . . ." (Ephesians 2:5b, 7, GNB). Amen.

---

1. Don Brown, *Tell a Tale of Iowa* (Des Moines, Iowa: Wallace-Homestead Book Company).

Chapter 21

❖❖❖❖❖❖❖

A Ten Week Strategy
For Improving Your Preaching

The following are suggestions which can help you keep your preaching edge by using the principles that have been listed in this book on preaching. There are specific suggestions for each of 10 weeks. In most cases you're asked to start doing something and then continue making it a part of your weekly routine.

This ten week regimen builds on former steps and each week is dependent on what you have done previously. It works best when kept in this order.

In most congregations it would be advisable to enlist a small group of lay people who represent various ages, educational backgrounds and financial status to help you in this improvement program. Invite them to come together, hand out this book, and explain the strategy. Ask that they be willing for ten weeks in a row to meet with you once a week and discuss how you're doing, how they can help, and the reactions of the congregation to your preaching. Go over chapter 17 discussing their opinions on the 16 suggestions. After you begin to have your sermons videotaped in the seventh week, you'll want to have that video on hand when the group gets together to critique and offer suggestions. If they were not there a particular Sunday to hear the sermon they can borrow the tape and preview it before coming to that meeting to give their advice.

Week number one: Begin by keeping a homiletic journal. See page 24 and 109 of this book. Start carrying the journal with you always and writing down those things you hear on the news, read in the paper, see in the movies, observe around you that might have the possibility one day of being the metaphor that will carry the gospel forward in the pulpit. Before you preach your sermon this first week, go into the pulpit where it will be delivered ahead of time and practice it out loud just as if the congregation were seated there listening to you. (See chapter 14 of this book.) Do this at least twice and preferably three times. Establish this rehearsal and keep the journal as a habit for the rest of the weeks.

Week number two: This week add to your sermon preparation the use of two or three runs (see page 131 of chapter 20 for a sample), one example of alliteration, and two words that would qualify in the speech technique called onomatopoeia (see page 85). This simply means using words that when pronounced, by their sound, help to reflect their meaning. Deliver a persuasive sermon on Sunday using this book's formula of a persuasive sermon based on congregational reaction (see chapter 6). Work hard on building a fire, a bridge, the focus, an example, your own witness, first steps and frame. Chapter 18 is an example.

Week number three: Prepare your sermon this week with special attention to inclusive language. Continue to use sermon runs, alliteration, and onomatopoeia. On Sunday deliver another audience reaction sermon. If you use a manuscript, it ought be the last time you take a completed manuscript into the pulpit! Assign one of your committee members to read chapter 15 and another member to read chapter 16 to make sure you are not a part of the pulpiteer family and that your sermon is wax free.

Week number four: Prepare very brief notes for your sermon delivery this week and be prepared to practice your sermon before delivering it using only those notes. When you deliver the sermon, be sure that you include your own faith story so that the congregation hears your witness and life experience with the gospel.

Week number five: During week five locate some local sources for historical stories about the community. See chapter 9 of this book for suggestions. And on Sunday, deliver a sermon based on local history which serves as the extended metaphor. Chapter 20 is a sample sermon. Your congregation is in for a treat and you will be delighted with their response.

Week number six: Check your sermon for opportunities to talk about money and stewardship. See chapter 11 of this book on "The Sermon On The Amount." Try delivering an extended narrative metaphor sermon. You'll find them explained in chapter 7 of this book. Pay special attention to the interest that your storytelling will generate as you deliver this sermon.

Week number seven: This week arrange to have your preaching videotaped. Do it on the following Sundays, also. And on Sunday do a sermon which includes the "whole gospel in twenty minutes." See page 107 of this book. This is one you might want to write out in manuscript style and have printed to hand out to the congregational members *after* the sermon is delivered. It's a sermon that you could advertise in the newspaper. This may attract people who have not been there before or very infrequently.

Week number eight: On Tuesday night of this week get a representative group from the congregation together to help you study the gospel appointed for the coming Sunday and make comments they're willing to have quoted by you from the pulpit about that gospel. That Sunday deliver a "people sermon" giving credit in the worship bulletin to those people who helped prepare the sermon and quoting them throughout (see page 111). Provide a brief questionnaire in the worship bulletin this Sunday asking people to give their suggestions about issues and gospel texts they would like to hear addressed from the pulpit. One of these suggestions might work for the next week.

Week number nine: Prepare a sermon on a cutting edge topic that's very hot in the community at that time. You might want to announce the subject ahead of time and that you'll be preaching about it next Sunday. See chapter 10 of this book for advice on how to go about it. On Sunday morning deliver your sermon on the controversial subject and let the people know that this is not an easy thing for you to do. Suggest you're simply seeking the wisdom of the scripture on the right or wrong in this situation.

Week number ten: Organize a group of seven or eight preaching partners this week and put them to work at once. See pages 110 to 112 of this book for suggestions. Sunday morning deliver a sermon on the gospel appointed for the day using the preaching partners forms they have provided to you. Announce that these partners will be helping you over the next six months and then a new group will be appointed to take their place. On this Sunday you might also want to provide a brief questionnaire about your preaching. You will want to quiz your original improvement committee to evaluate how the ten week preaching improvement strategy has or hasn't worked.

If you have worked very diligently and have had a committee that was serious about its task of supervising you, you are bound to have improved in your preaching over this ten week period. A conscientious preacher who finishes this regimen could probably be described as one who keeps a homiletical journal and thus always has a wealth of examples and metaphors to use, a preacher who practices sermons out loud ahead of time and thus is very confident and effective in the pulpit, and a preacher whose preparation is so thorough that he/she uses techniques such as runs, alliteration, and other good rhetorical practices. This preacher could also be described as delivering sermons that are very interesting as well as theologically correct and are based on how a typical audience listens to a verbal presentation. This preacher varies the type of sermon from week to week and uses inclusive language so that everyone feels an integral part of the congregation. This preacher preaches from brief notes and thus has good eye contact with the congregation and involves his/her own witness to the faith in the presentation. These preachers own the history and culture of their community and delight their congregation with intriguing stories about it. Their preaching is close to the ground as they address money and stewardship issues and very controversial subjects. They often deliver their sermons using the extended metaphor which commands attention and reveals the preacher as poetic as well as literary. They have the bigger picture as you hear something of the whole gospel in each sermon and they are in touch with the real life of their sermon hearers as they seek input from the congregational members.

The above sounds like the ideal preacher and I'm sure any lay person reading this would say that it is. If this sounds like a lot to accomplish, don't be discouraged. Fosdick, one of the all-time great preachers, said:

> *Of course, nothing can make preaching easy. At best it means drenching a congregation with one's life blood.*

But while, like all high work, it involves severe concentration, toil, and self-expenditure, it can be so exhilarating as to recreate in the preacher the strength it takes, as good agriculture replaces the soil it uses.[1]

Ten Basic Questions In Establishing
The Preacher's Edge In Sermon Content

1. Is the scripture well-represented as the basis for the message?
2. Will my first few words get the congregation's attention?
3. Did I include some good humor related to the theme?
4. Have I represented both sexes as equals? (See endnote[2])
5. Have I shared my own faith and did I include myself as part of the listeners?
6. Is there a specific "so what" which invites us to *do* because of this sermon?
7. Is there a strong central focus?
8. Will this sermon give hope and lift us up?
9. Did I address all ages, colors, educational levels and financial status?
10. Is the whole gospel to be heard in this sermon?

I recommend that you test your sermon after it is completed and before you deliver it with the above questions. There are many more one could ask but these will attend to certain basic elements that need to be there as we preach for this generation of listeners.

In the preface to his book on *The Mystery of Preaching*, James Black wrote:

In spite of all the advice I have tried to crush within these covers, great preaching will always remain a mystery, not least to the preacher himself. It is bound up ultimately in the greater mystery of personality.[3]

---

1. Lionel George Crocker, *1897 Harry Emerson Fosdick's Art of Preaching: An Anthology.* Edited and compiled by Lionel Crocker (Springfield, IL: Thomas, 1971), p. 59.

2. "Suffice it to say that the male pastor who does use inclusive language, who does acknowledge the validity of the issue, has taken a political stand that will be noticed and supported by those in the congregation who are struggling with the need for new roles for women. Conversely, any male pastor who does not make changes in his language is also communicating a political message of support for the traditional oppressive arrangement, whether he is conscious of this or not. The congregation will be quite aware of either message . . . the preacher has no choice but to take a stand . . . a male pastor who thinks he is quite liberating in his preaching and yet whose language remains unreconstructed will find that a certain skepticism greets his statements, whereas a pastor who does use altered language will be given the benefit of the doubt by those women who feel oppressed." From: Justo Gonzalez and Catherine Gunsalus Gonzalez, *Liberation Preaching: The Pulpit and the Oppressed* (Nashville: Abingdon Preacher's Library, 1980), p. 98.

3. James Black, *The Mystery of Preaching* (London: Marshall, Morgan, and Scott, 1924. Revised edition, 1977), p. iii.